NORTH STAR

LISTENING AND SPEAKING

Basic/Low Intermediate

SECOND EDITION

Robin Mills
Laurie Frazier

Series Editors
Frances Boyd
Carol Numrich

Longman

NorthStar: Listening and Speaking, Basic/Low Intermediate, Second Edition
Teacher's Manual and Achievement Tests

Pearson Education, 10 Bank Street, White Plains, NY 10606

Teacher's Manual by Beth Maher
Achievement Tests by Evelyn Fella

Test consultant: Tay Lesley

Development director: Penny Laporte
Project manager: Debbie Sistino
Development editor: Françoise Leffler
Vice president, director of design and production: Rhea Banker
Executive managing editor: Linda Moser
Production editor: Marc Oliver
Production manager: Liza Pleva
Production coordinator: Melissa Leyva
Director of manufacturing: Patrice Fraccio
Senior manufacturing buyer: Dave Dickey
Cover design: Rhea Banker
Text design: Quorum Creative Services
Text composition: TSI Graphics
Text font: 11/13 Sabon

ISBN 0-201-78844-6

Printed in the United States of America
4 5 6 7 8 9 10—TCS—09 08 07 06 05

Contents

Teacher's Manual

Achievement Tests

Introduction to the *NorthStar* Series

The *NorthStar* Approach to Language Teaching   *NorthStar* is a five-level, integrated skills series for language learning. The series is divided into two strands: listening and speaking, and reading and writing. There are five books in each strand, taking students from the high beginning level of the *Introductory Student Book* to the advanced level of the *Advanced Student Book*. At each level, the two strands explore different aspects of the same contemporary themes. Each book practices language-learning skills through high-interest thematic content.

In addition to the Student Books, the *Writing Activity Book* for each level of the reading and writing strand expands and reinforces the writing process. The *Audio Program* includes, on CD or cassette, all the reading and listening segments as well as pronunciation exercises. The *Video Program* includes 3- to 5-minute segments for each unit. The segments are thematically linked to the units in the Student Books to offer additional material for listening comprehension and discussion or writing.

Integrated skills are at the heart of the *NorthStar* series. When two or more language skills are integrated, language learning is apt to be more authentic, natural, and motivating. Integrating skills offers more opportunity for recycling and reinforcing key vocabulary, grammatical structures, and ideas. As a result, students have more occasions to assimilate information and language, thereby facilitating learning.

Approach to Reading and Writing   *NorthStar* supports the approach that learning to be a good writer means learning to be a good reader and vice versa. Reading skills are taught *implicitly* throughout each unit. For example, the comprehension exercises are designed to give practice in reading skills, such as predicting, identifying main ideas and details, skimming and scanning.

Writing skills are taught *implicitly* through the readings: The readings serve as models of good writing. In the Style section, writing skills are taught *explicitly* through analysis, explanation, and guided practice.

The writing process begins at the start of each unit (often with the first Prediction exercise), continues through the unit (with dialogues, written reactions to a partner's comments, chart completion, note taking), includes the Style section (with explicit writing skills and structured practice), and culminates in the Writing Topics section, where students are asked to produce a complete piece of writing.

Reading and writing skills—including strategies for improving vocabulary, comprehension, and grammar—are cultivated in every section of every unit. In the Research Topics section, the reading and writing integration becomes most clear and relevant, as students are asked to conduct research and read texts from a variety of authentic sources and then integrate ideas from these sources into their own writing.

Approach to Listening and Speaking   *NorthStar* provides structured opportunities for students to practice listening to many types of discourse. Listening skills are taught *implicitly* throughout each unit. For example, the comprehension exercises are designed to give practice in such listening skills as predicting, identifying main ideas and details, and note taking.

Speaking skills are taught *implicitly* through the listenings: The listenings serve as models of functional language or conventional style. In the Style section, speaking skills are taught *explicitly* though analysis, explanation, a carefully structured pronunciation syllabus, and guided practice. The teaching of speaking begins at the start of each unit (often with the first Prediction exercise), continues through the unit (with categorizing and ranking activities, interviews, games, pronunciation practice, comparing answers and discussing differences, sharing opinions), includes the Style section (with explicit functional skills and structured practice), and culminates in the Speaking Topics section, where students use their speaking skills to create role plays, case studies, debates, radio announcements, and presentations.

Listening and speaking skills—including learning strategies for improving vocabulary, comprehension, and grammar—are cultivated in every section of every unit. In the Research Topics section, the listening and speaking integration becomes most clear and relevant as students are asked to conduct projects such as surveys or in-person and telephone interviews and then integrate ideas from these sources into their own oral presentations.

Approach to Grammar   Content drives the organization of the grammar syllabus. Accordingly, students have opportunities to encounter and work with grammar structures in authentic contexts. The purpose of the Grammar section is to enable clear and accurate discussion and writing about the unit theme.

The Grammar section of each unit is not intended to be an exhaustive treatment of a grammatical point. Rather, it is an opportunity for students to focus on a new or familiar point within the specific context of the unit. Teachers and students can use the Grammar section either as the first step in presenting a particular structure or as a review. For more detailed explanations of the grammar points, a chart of Grammar Book References is included in the Student Books. This chart cross-references the unit grammar to appropriate sections in two successful grammar series: Azar's grammar series and *Focus on Grammar*.

Grammar is taught both inductively (through discovery) and deductively (through explanation). First, students answer questions to discover the form, usage, and meaning of the grammar. Next, they read an explanation of the point, with examples in the thematic context of the unit. Finally, students practice the structures in exercises related to the content of the unit.

Approach to Vocabulary   Vocabulary practice has been increased in the Second Edition of *NorthStar.* Vocabulary is taught both *directly* and *indirectly.* Specific vocabulary exercises focus on meaning, usage, and word forms. In many of the other exercises (grammar, style, speaking and writing topics, research), the vocabulary reappears but is not the focus of the exercise.

In Section 1, Focus on the Topic, vocabulary has been chosen for its relevance in discussing the topic/theme. In other cases, the vocabulary is essential for comprehension of a listening or reading text, so the focus becomes preteaching vocabulary for comprehension. In Section 3, Focus on Vocabulary, the work takes on a different focus, as words are reviewed and studied in more depth. In this section, students are asked to go beyond the vocabulary presented in the text and explore new items. In the listening and speaking strand, a particular effort has been made to focus on idiomatic and informal expressions that are common in spoken English.

Correction in Oral Work

Students with academic and/or career goals need and want correction. You should listen to what students are saying on two levels: form and content. Use correction to help students close the gap between what they want to say and what they are able to say. Cued self-correction is preferable. Self-correction can be promoted in several ways. You will want to vary your strategies depending on the activity and time available.

- **On-the-spot correction:** As students are talking, you can use a nonverbal gesture (such as raising a finger, pulling an earlobe, writing the error on the board) to indicate that a correction is necessary.

- **Individual notes:** You may want to write down individual student's errors on a chart to have them corrected when the activity is finished. For example, in the Sample Error Chart below, general feedback is on the left-hand side. You can use symbols such as ↑ to mean "above average," → to mean "average," and ↓ to mean "below average." Specific feedback is on the right-hand side. An index card, divided into three equal parts, also works well.

Name *Maria R*	Class *English 101*	
General Feedback Fluency ↑ Accuracy → Pronunciation ↓	**Pronunciation/Stress** *these* /ð/ *think* /θ/	**Grammar/Vocabulary** *Yesterday, they say* . . . *The students works together* . . .
Notes *Interesting ideas about education.* *Be sure to speak loudly, too.* *Eye contact was much better.*	*rural* /r/ *official* *product*	*They have much problems* . . . *They needed a material subject.*

- **Collective notes:** You may want to take notes that can be used later to create an error-correction exercise.

- **Tapes and transcriptions:** You may want to use tapes and transcriptions to increase students' awareness of language errors. Audiotaping student conversations and reports is especially useful in the pronunciation activities in Sections 4A and 4D, where students have an opportunity for extensive oral production. First, tape the conversation, role play, or report; then record your feedback, modeling correct pronunciation. You can also transcribe a portion for use as an error-correction activity. Use blanks or underscoring to indicate errors; then have students correct their mistakes and encourage them to appreciate how their language is improving. Occasionally, it may be interesting to have students transcribe small bits of their own language for the same purpose.

If possible, you may want to videotape an activity. Play it back and elicit oral and written comments about students' own language and their feelings about seeing themselves speaking English. Follow this with some error correction on the board.

- **Fluency line:** Students need to develop fluency. The following activity develops fluency by giving students a chance to repeat the same story, explanation, or opinion to several different people.

  Divide the class in half. Have Group B students line up, side by side, and then have Group A students line up opposite them. Each Group A student then tells the Group B student opposite him or her a story, explanation, or opinion, depending on the assignment. Time the Group A students, giving them a set amount of time to talk. The Group A students must not stop talking, and the Group B students must not interrupt, except to ask for clarification. When you signal, all Group A students must take a step to the right and repeat their comments to their next Group B partner. (The Group A student at the end of the line has to walk around to the far left to find his or her new partner.) The activity continues with you signaling each partner to change. You can speed up the process by incrementally reducing the amount of time between partners. At a designated point, the roles are reversed so that Group B students have an opportunity to talk, and Group A students have an opportunity to listen.

  The format of this activity can be modified. For example, you could have students line up in concentric circles instead of lines or have them walk freely around the room, talking with different partners.

- **Audio journal:** An audio journal is like a written journal except that students record their ideas on an audio cassette tape instead of on paper. There are a number of assignments that can lead to audio journals—for example, comments on topics discussed in class, reports on individual research, and first drafts of oral presentations. Some teachers like to have students record pronunciation exercises as a way to individualize error correction. For all these activities, it is important to specify how long the students should speak and whether they should read prepared comments or speak extemporaneously. When you receive the audio journals, you can give students feedback by recording a reply right after their comments. When replying, be sure to discuss both content and form.

A Message from the Series Editors

We think of a good textbook as a musical score or a movie script. It tells you the moves and roughly how quickly and in what sequence to make them. But until you and your students bring it to life, a book is silent and static, a mere possibility. We hope that *NorthStar* orients, guides, and interests you as teachers.

It is our hope that the *NorthStar* series stimulates your students' thinking, which in turn stimulates their language learning, and that they will have many opportunities to reflect on the viewpoints of journalists, commentators, researchers, other students, and people in the community. Further, we hope that *NorthStar* guides them to develop their own point of view on the many and varied themes encompassed by this series.

We welcome your comments and questions. Please send them to us at the publisher:

Frances Boyd and Carol Numrich, Series Editors
NorthStar
Pearson Education
10 Bank Street
White Plains, NY 10606

Overview of the *Teacher's Manual and Achievement Tests*

The *NorthStar Teacher's Manual* includes:

- Specific suggestions for teaching each unit, including:
    - ✓ Unit-by-unit overview (scope and sequence) and summary
    - ✓ Unit-by-unit description of the Focus, Setup, and Expansion/Homework activities for each exercise
    - ✓ Suggested teaching times
    - ✓ Cross-references to the companion strand, Grammar Book References, *Writing Activity Book,* Video, and Companion Website
- The Answer Key to the Student Book
- Reproducible Achievement Tests with Answer Keys—including the test audioscript and test audio CD for the *Listening and Speaking* strand; and a test-generating CD-ROM to allow teachers to customize and adapt the 300 test items and writing tasks on the Reading and Writing Achievement Tests for the *Reading and Writing* strand
- An alphabetized-by-unit word list of the key vocabulary items practiced in each unit

COURSE PLANNER

Each unit contains approximately eight hours of classroom material, plus expansion, homework, and support material. Teachers can customize the units by assigning some exercises for homework and/or eliminating others. To help teachers customize the units for their specific teaching situation, the Unit-by-Unit Teaching Suggestions in the *Teacher's Manual* include 1, 2, or 3 stars to indicate the relative importance of each section or exercise:

> ✪✪✪ **Essential** sections
> ✪✪ **Recommended** sections
> ✪ **Optional** sections

To use *NorthStar* most effectively, see the teaching guide below.

CLASS TIME AVAILABLE PER UNIT	SECTIONS TO COMPLETE
8 hours or more	Essential (✪✪✪), Recommended (✪✪), Optional (✪)
6 hours	Essential (✪✪✪), Recommended (✪✪)
4 hours	Essential (✪✪✪) only

Offbeat Jobs

OVERVIEW

Theme:	Work
Listenings:	Listening One: *What's My Job?* (a game show) Listening Two: *More Offbeat Jobs* (a report on an unusual website)
Critical Thinking Skills:	Classify information Rank personal values and preferences in work Relate personal skills to job responsibilities Infer word meaning from context Infer situational context Support opinions with information from the interviews Assess a person's character and recommend a job
Listening Tasks:	Listen and predict Listen for main ideas Listen for details Interpret speaker's tone and attitude Sort information from the interview Relate listenings to personal experience Synthesize information from both listenings
Speaking Tasks:	Make predictions Express and defend opinions Act out a conversation Make small talk Interview a classmate Brainstorm offbeat jobs Report research findings
Pronunciation:	Stress patterns of nouns and adjectives
Vocabulary:	Context clues Dictionary work Word definitions
Grammar:	Descriptive adjectives

UNIT SUMMARY

This unit is about uncommon jobs and job satisfaction as well as the interests and skills people bring to their work. Listening One is an excerpt of a game show in which a contestant must guess a person's job. Listening Two features short personal statements by a window washer and a professional shopper.

The companion unit of *NorthStar: Reading and Writing* deals with finding satisfying work by identifying important personal and job characteristics.

1 Focus on the Topic, PAGE 1

✪✪✪ A PREDICTING

Suggested Time: 10 minutes ⏱

Focus
To invite students to think about unusual work situations.

Setup
Have students study the pictures and the title, then take a moment or two to think about the questions before discussing them. As students answer the questions, write the answers on the board to encourage broad participation.

Expansion/Homework
(1) Have students work in pairs or share answers in small groups, then report their ideas to the class. (2) You may want to ask students their ideas about common and unusual (offbeat) jobs. List them on the board.

✪✪ B SHARING INFORMATION

Suggested Time: 20 minutes ⏱

Focus
To focus students' attention on criteria that are important in job selection.

Setup
Ask students to complete the questionnaire individually, then discuss their answers in small groups. Encourage students to talk about how important each item is to them personally.

Expansion/Homework
(1) In pairs, students interview each other about how important each item is, using questions such as *How important is the salary to you?* or *How important are work hours?* Circulate, helping students as necessary with questions and vocabulary. (2) Write the seven items on the board. Ask how many students

thought salary was the most important criteria and write the number next to the item. Continue for the remaining six items. Encourage students to discuss what they agree and disagree on.

Link to *NorthStar: Reading and Writing*
If students are also using the companion text, you may want to have them use the list of criteria from Section 1B in the listening/speaking text to generate a questionnaire similar to Section 1B in the reading/writing text.

✪✪✪ C | **PREPARING TO LISTEN**

BACKGROUND
Suggested Time: 20–25 minutes 🕐

Focus
To give students more information about offbeat jobs.

Setup
Have students read the chart and the list of job titles. Answer any questions that arise. Have students complete the chart individually, then discuss what they have written with another student. Then have students answer the questions on their own and compare and discuss their answers with a partner.

Expansion/Homework
(1) Students can complete this exercise as a class. (2) You may want to assign this section as homework. Then have students discuss their answers in pairs or small groups.

VOCABULARY FOR COMPREHENSION
Suggested Time: 15 minutes 🕐

Focus
To introduce vocabulary and concepts related to work in the food industry in preparation for the listening.

Setup
Have students read the sentences and match the definitions individually, then compare their answers with a partner (of similar fluency).

Expansion/Homework
(1) Have students read sentences and answers out loud; then discuss vocabulary in the context of the students' native cultures and everyday lives. For example, discuss factories and jobs, game shows they may watch or that may be popular, what common/offbeat jobs they have heard of, what kinds of food flavors and tastes they like, and so on. (2) You may want to assign this section as homework, then have students discuss their answers in pairs or small groups.

2 Focus on Listening, PAGE 5

✪✪✪ A | LISTENING ONE: *What's My Job?*

Suggested Time: 10 minutes ⏱

Focus
To establish the context and tone of the listening text: game show, host, contestant; to elicit predictions about the content of the show.

Setup
Have students read the questions, listen to the text, then select and compare their answers.

✪✪✪ LISTENING FOR MAIN IDEAS

Suggested Time: 10 minutes ⏱

Focus
To help students listen for the main ideas about Peter's offbeat job (ice-cream taster).

Setup
Have the students read the statements, then circle the correct answer as they listen. To help concentration, invite students to close their eyes during the listening. Have students compare their answers to those of a partner, then check them as a class. If they disagree, have them give reasons for their answers.

✪✪✪ LISTENING FOR DETAILS

Suggested Time: 15 minutes ⏱

Focus
To get students to listen carefully again, this time for specific information about Peter's job.

Setup
First, have students read the sentences, marking the ones they already know are true or false. Play the segment again, letting students compare answers after every two or three items. If disagreements arise, replay the segment rather than simply giving the answer.

Expansion/Homework
Have students correct the false statements.

Link to *NorthStar: Reading and Writing*
If students are also using the companion text, you may want to have them use the questions raised in Reading One to talk about Peter: *What does he like to do? What does he do well? What is his job setting like? What are his job rewards?*

✪✪ REACTING TO THE LISTENING
Suggested Time: 20 minutes

Focus
To encourage students to make inferences based on tone of voice and word choice; to encourage students to listen beyond the literal meaning of the words.

Setup
For Exercise 1, have students read the questions, then listen to Excerpt One. As a class, discuss questions 1 and 2. Ask students to listen for the tone of voice and notice how it affects meaning. Have students do Excerpt Two and Three on their own. Discuss as a class. For Exercise 2, give students time to read and think about their answers. Discuss answers as a class.

Expansion/Homework
(1) Have students work in pairs for Exercise 1 and discuss the questions in Exercise 2 in small groups. (2) In Excerpt Two, the host says, "Gee, that sounds like a difficult job, Peter." Play that excerpt again. Have students listen to the sarcastic tone. Discuss its meaning. Then, have students role-play saying the same line in an earnest voice. A bitter voice. A sad/serious voice. Try the same exercise with the simple phrase, "I'm OK." Demonstrate different meanings of "I'm OK" using tone and facial expressions as well as body language.

✪✪✪ B | LISTENING TWO: *More Offbeat Jobs*
Suggested Time: 5 minutes

Focus
To add to students' understanding of less common jobs and job satisfaction; to give students practice listening to short pieces with different voices.

Setup
For Exercise 1, have students answer the questions about the photos in small groups or as a class. Then play the tape and invite students to complete Exercise 2, then check their answers in pairs. Play the tape again so students can complete the chart in Exercise 3. Walk around the room and assist as needed.

Expansion/Homework
You may want to have students listen to the tape once and then complete the exercises individually. They can share answers, then listen to the tape again to confirm their answers.

✪✪✪ C | LINKING LISTENINGS ONE AND TWO
Suggested Time: 15 minutes

Focus
To get students to express opinions about the jobs featured in Listenings One and Two.

Setup

Have students think about how they would answer the questions, then divide the class into small groups to discuss their answers. The small groups can report the highlights of the discussion to the class, which you can note on the board.

Expansion/Homework

(1) Work with the whole class, getting students to listen and respond to one another's ideas. Encourage the use of vocabulary from Section 1C by listing it on the board and referring students to it. Correct pronunciation and usage errors orally and on the board. (2) You may want to have groups of students prepare their thoughts for homework, then report to the class and discuss their opinions.

Link to *NorthStar: Reading and Writing*

If the students are also using the companion text, you may want to have them write answers for the ice-cream taster, the window washer, and the professional shopper following the format in Section 2C of that text.

3 Focus on Vocabulary, PAGE 9

✪ EXERCISE 1
Suggested Time: 10 minutes ⏱

Focus

To work with unit vocabulary in context by using these new words in conversation.

Setup

Have the students fill in the blanks on their own. Then work in pairs, comparing answers and practicing the dialog.

Expansion/Homework

Assign for homework and check answers with a partner in class. Practice dialog with a partner in class.

✪ EXERCISE 2
Suggested Time: 15 minutes ⏱

Focus

To work with unit vocabulary in context by using these new words in conversation.

Setup

In pairs, have students respond to the conversational starter using the vocabulary words provided.

Expansion/Homework

Have students write out responses for homework. In class, they can check their answers with a partner and role-play the dialogs.

Link to *NorthStar: Reading and Writing*
Provide students with a vocabulary list from Section 1C in the companion text. Encourage them to use these vocabulary words in their answers as well. Have each pair of students select one of the items from this exercise and create a longer dialog that uses as many of the vocabulary words from both texts as possible. Invite the pair that uses the most words in a single dialog to share their dialog with the class.

 For extra vocabulary practice, have students work on the self-grading vocabulary activities for the unit on the NorthStar Companion Website at **http://www.longman.com/northstar**.

4 Focus on Speaking, PAGE 11

✪✪A PRONUNCIATION: Stress

Suggested Time: 30 minutes 🕐

Focus
To develop awareness and provide practice of appropriate syllable and word stress.

Setup
Have students listen to the examples on the tape. Then they can listen to and complete Exercise 1. Students can show what they have marked to a partner before listening again for stress. After the second listening, go over the answers as a class. For Exercise 2, have students work in pairs and show each other the answers after a bit of practice. For Exercise 3, have students work with a different partner. One student asks using the phrases on the left. The other student answers using the correct words on the right. They should change roles when they have completed the exercise. Circulate as necessary to help with pronunciation and appropriate stress.

Expansion/Homework
After students complete Exercise 2, have them brainstorm a list of words. Write them on the board. Then have students practice pronouncing these words with appropriate stress, first as a class, then individually.

Link to *NorthStar: Reading and Writing*
If students are also using the companion text, you may want to have them practice syllable stress with the words in Section 3 of that text. Try giving students rubber bands to stretch as they pronounce the lengthened syllable.

✪✪✪ B STYLE: Small Talk   o

Suggested Time: 20 minutes 🕐

Focus
To help students engage in small talk, especially about other people's jobs and interests.

Setup
Read the introductory statement and the phrases in the box aloud to the class. Divide the students into pairs to complete the conversation.

Expansion/Homework
(1) You may want to use a fluency line (see page viii) with students. (2) You could ask students to make a chart. Across the top of a blank sheet of paper they should write three questions: *What's your name? What do you do? What do you like to do?* Down the left side they can make a list of students in the class. Have them walk around the room and talk to other students to complete the chart.

Link to *NorthStar: Reading and Writing*
If students are also using the companion text, you may want to have them assume the role of one of the three characters in Reading Two. Then practice this conversation.

✪✪ C GRAMMAR: Descriptive Adjectives

Suggested Time: 25 minutes 🕐

Focus
To have students practice using descriptive adjectives to talk about jobs.

Setup
In Exercise 1, have students read the examples, then answer the questions. Ask them to read the grammar box silently. For Exercise 2, have students work in pairs (of similar language ability). Have two students read the example so that the roles are clear: one makes a statement, the other comments. Walk around and cue students to correct their own errors in grammar, vocabulary, and pronunciation. Remind them to take turns.

Expansion/Homework
(1) For Exercise 2, you may want to have students brainstorm a list of jobs. Write them on the board. As a class write appropriate descriptive adjectives for these job titles. Ask students to write sentences using these words. (2) For further practice, offer exercises from *Focus on Grammar, Basic* and from *Basic English Grammar*. See the Grammar Book References on page 167 of the Student Book for specific units and chapters.

Link to *NorthStar: Reading and Writing*
If students are also using the companion text, you may want to have them use the e-mails in Sections 3 and 4B (Exercise 1) of that text as models for writing a

new e-mail from either the ice-cream taster, the window washer, or the professional shopper.

 For extra listening practice, have students use the NorthStar Companion Video.

✪✪✪ D SPEAKING TOPICS

Suggested Time: 25–30 minutes

Focus
To extend students' ability to interview and discuss jobs, especially in a less controlled situation.

Setup
Read the directions to students. Have students work on the chart with a partner (sitting next to them). Before doing Step 2, have students brainstorm different kinds of jobs. Write these words on the board for students to refer to while doing Step 2. Students can do Step 3 as a class. Be sure that they understand that they are to listen for students whose skills and interests are similar to their own and write down this information.

Expansion/Homework
After students have completed Step 2, group students of similar inclination together and have them discuss what they do with their particular skills and interests.

Link to *NorthStar: Reading and Writing*
If students are also using the companion text, you may want to have them use the e-mails in Sections 3 and 4B of that text as the basis for a role play. One student is Jenny, the other Cristina. Encourage Jenny to ask questions. Cristina answers according to the information in the e-mails.

✪ E RESEARCH TOPIC

Suggested Time: 30–50 minutes in class, 1–2 hours outside

Focus
To have students go outside the class and do research on a particular job.

Setup
Before completing the activity, brainstorm with students about where they could go for information. Then students can go to the library or look on the Internet to get information. When they have found the information, they can report back to the class about it. While students are listening to their classmates' reports, encourage them to listen for which job sounds most interesting, most stressful, and any other criteria you establish.

Expansion/Homework
(1) Students can give reports in small groups, then report back to the class on the listening task. (2) You may want to have students work in pairs, rather than individually. Get listeners to ask a few questions (put cues on index cards).

A Piece of the Country in the City

OVERVIEW	
Theme:	The Country and the City
Listenings:	Listening One: *Community Gardens* (a radio interview) Listening Two: *Let's Hear from Our Listener* (a radio call-in show)
Critical Thinking Skills:	Classify information Compare and contrast city and country life Interpret a graph Infer word meaning from context Infer situational context Categorize sounds
Listening Tasks:	Listen and predict Listen and identify main ideas Listen for details Interpret speaker's tone and attitude Relate listenings to own community Summarize information from the two listenings Listen to and take notes on student reports
Speaking Tasks:	Make predictions Share opinions Role-play Express agreement with *too* and *not either* Make past tense statements Act out a scripted conversation and news report Talk about favorite places Report observations on local urban greening
Pronunciation:	Regular verbs in the simple past tense
Vocabulary:	Context clues Word definitions
Grammar:	Simple past tense

UNIT SUMMARY

This unit deals with the development of green areas and community gardens in urban areas. Listening One is a radio interview about community gardens, satisfactions, and problems. Listening Two features a radio talk-show segment on what people do to keep cities clean and green.

The companion unit of *NorthStar: Reading and Writing* compares life in the city with life in the country.

1 Focus on the Topic, PAGE 17

✪✪✪ A PREDICTING

Suggested Time: 10 minutes ⏱

Focus
To get students thinking about the differences between the city, the suburbs, and the country.

Setup
After students study the picture and the title, have them think about the questions before discussing them. Make sure students understand the key words: *city, suburb,* and *country.* As students offer answers to questions, write their answers on the board to encourage broad participation.

Expansion/Homework
(1) Have students work in pairs or share their answers in small groups, then report their ideas to the class. (2) You may want to ask students about the area where they live. Can they identify nearby cities, suburbs, and rural areas?

✪✪ B SHARING INFORMATION

Suggested Time: 20 minutes ⏱

Focus
To focus student's attention on specific differences between urban, suburban, and rural areas, and to give them vocabulary to discuss their differences.

Setup
Have students discuss the questions in small groups.

Expansion/Homework
You may want to have groups share highlights of their discussion with the class.

✪✪✪ C **PREPARING TO LISTEN**

BACKGROUND
Suggested Time: 15 minutes 🕐

Focus
To introduce students to the concept of urban greening and an example of urban greening: community gardens.

Setup
Have students read the graph about city/country population in the United States and answer the questions. Discuss the answers as a class. Have students read the paragraphs on their own. Have them work on the chart in small groups. Discuss the answers as a class.

Expansion/Homework
(1) You could assign this section as homework and discuss the answers in class.
(2) After they have finished the exercise, you may want to create new groups and have students read their answers to each other.

Link to *NorthStar: Reading and Writing*
If students are also using the companion text, you may want to extend the discussion of gardens and community gardens to include where students lived when they were children, as in Section 1B of that text.

VOCABULARY FOR COMPREHENSION
Suggested Time: 15 minutes 🕐

Focus
To introduce vocabulary and concepts related to gardening in an urban environment in preparation for the listening.

Setup
Have students complete the exercise individually, then compare answers with a partner.

Expansion/Homework
(1) You may want to have students complete the exercise, then share answers as a class. (2) You may want to assign the exercise as homework.

Link to *NorthStar: Reading and Writing*
If students are also using the companion text, you may want to have them write the vocabulary from Section 1C of both texts in a notebook. You may wish to have them include vocabulary from Section 1B of the listening/speaking text as well. This list of the combined vocabulary items can be used later in the unit when activities call for it.

2 Focus on Listening, PAGE 21

✪✪✪ A LISTENING ONE: *Community Gardens*

Suggested Time: 10 minutes ⏱

Focus
To establish the context and tone of a radio news show; to familiarize students with the speaker; to elicit predictions about the content of the listening segment.

Setup
Have students read the questions and choose the correct answers as they listen. Discuss answers as a class.

Expansion/Homework
Have students work on these in small groups. You can encourage these groups to share what they know about community gardens.

✪✪✪ LISTENING FOR MAIN IDEAS

Suggested Time: 15 minutes ⏱

Focus
To help students listen for the main ideas: the reasons for creating a community garden.

Setup
Have the students read the statements, then write their answers as they listen. To help concentration, invite students to close their eyes during some of the listening. Have students read their answers to a partner, then check them as a class.

Expansion/Homework
You may want to have students fill in their answers, then read them to the class, inviting a variety of responses.

✪✪✪ LISTENING FOR DETAILS

Suggested Time: 15 minutes ⏱

Focus
To get students to listen carefully again, this time for specific information.

Setup
First, have students read the sentences, checking off the ones they already know are true. Play the news report again, letting students compare answers after every two or three items. If disagreements arise, replay the segment, rather than simply giving the answer.

Expansion/Homework
Have students correct the sentences that aren't true.

Link to *NorthStar: Reading and Writing*

If students are also using the companion text, you may want to have them reread Reading One. In small groups have students discuss the following questions: *Do you think Zachary Blaine would change his mind if he knew that kids growing up in the city could participate in a community garden? Does it change your opinion about whether it's better to raise a family in the city or the country?*

✪✪ REACTING TO THE LISTENING
Suggested Time: 15 minutes 🕐

Focus

To encourage students to make inferences based on tone of voice and word choice; to encourage students to listen beyond the literal meaning of the words. Also, to have students discuss their own reactions to the material.

Setup

For Exercise 1, have students read the questions. While listening to the excerpts, have students select their answers. Discuss the answers as a class. Probe for reasons for students' choices. Help students focus on how the man speaks rather than simply on what he says. For Exercise 2, give students time to read the questions and think about their answers. Discuss as a class.

Expansion/Homework

(1) You could break students into small groups, asking them to reach a group decision for answers to the questions in Exercise 1 and discuss their responses to questions in Exercise 2. (2) Have students choose one of the questions from Exercise 2. For homework, have them write a paragraph explaining their answer. The following day in class, put students who answered the same question in small groups together to discuss their ideas. This should make for a richer discussion because the students have been given time to formulate their ideas.

✪✪✪ B   LISTENING TWO: *Let's Hear from Our Listeners*
Suggested Time: 15 minutes 🕐

Focus

To increase students' understanding of urban greening and beautification; to listen to a radio call-in show with different voices.

Setup

First, have students work with a partner to answer the "Before you listen" questions about the illustrations. Then have them listen to the segment and fill in the "After you listen" portion of the chart. Students can read their answers out loud to a partner.

Expansion/Homework

You may want to have students complete the whole chart by themselves, then compare answers with those of a partner. Elicit a variety of responses to "Before you listen" from the whole class.

✪✪✪ C | **LINKING LISTENINGS ONE AND TWO**

Suggested Time: 15 minutes 🕐

Focus
To get students to integrate the ideas from Listenings One and Two.

Setup
Have students work in groups of three to complete the chart. Share highlights with the class.

Expansion/Homework
(1) Work with the whole class, getting students to listen and respond to one another's ideas. Encourage the use of vocabulary from Section 1 by listing it on the board and referring students to it. (2) You could assign this as homework and discuss it in class the following day. (3) Have students discuss examples of urban greening where they are living now. Ask: *Are urban greening and beautification necessary for the community you live in? What else can be done to save nature? What can you do to make your school, work, and home environments greener?*

3 Focus on Vocabulary, PAGE 24

✪ **EXERCISE 1**
Suggested Time: 10 minutes 🕐

Focus
To work with unit vocabulary in context by matching definitions.

Setup
Students can complete this exercise individually, then read their answers out loud to a partner or to the class.

Expansion/Homework
This can be assigned for homework. Ask students to check their own answers by checking a dictionary.

✪ **EXERCISE 2**
Suggested Time: 10 minutes 🕐

Focus
To practice new words from the unit by using them in oral dialog exercise.

Setup
Have students work alone to complete the conversation. Then, have the students practice reading the conversation in pairs (of different fluency levels). One student is A; the other student is B. Remind them to switch roles. Correct pronunciation and intonation.

Expansion/Homework

(1) Assign this for homework. In class, have students practice the dialog in pairs while you circulate checking pronunciation. (2) You may want to divide the class into two groups: one-half reads the part of A, the other half reads the part of B.

✪ EXERCISE 3
Suggested Time: 15 minutes 🕐

Focus

To have students practice using the vocabulary presented in this unit in a role play.

Setup

Have students work in pairs taking turns assuming the roles of city official and neighbor. Walk around the room helping students to get the role-play going, to correct pronunciation and usage.

Expansion/Homework

(1) Have students listen to a few of these dialogs, then in pairs have them write five sentences that explain why urban greening programs are good for cities. (2) If class time permits, encourage students to brainstorm more ideas about making the neighborhood greener and more beautiful. They can then use these ideas to extend the conversation.

Link to *NorthStar: Reading and Writing*

If students are using the companion text, you may want to have them use the vocabulary from Section 3 of both texts to write sentences about the area in which they live.

 For extra vocabulary practice, have students work on the self-grading vocabulary activities for the unit on the NorthStar Companion Website at **http://www.longman.com/northstar**.

4 Focus on Speaking, PAGE 26

✪✪A   PRONUNCIATION: Pronunciation of Past Tense

Suggested Time: 20 minutes 🕐

Focus

To practice pronunciation of *-ed*, the past tense marker, in the context of community gardens.

Setup

Have students read the rules and do the exercises. They can read what they have written to a partner or a small group of students (from different language backgrounds, if possible) to expose them to a variety of pronunciation possibilities). Circulate, as necessary, to help with pronunciation.

Expansion/Homework

After students complete Exercise 3, you may want to have them share these verbs as a class. Encourage students to think of more regular verbs. Write them on the board. Then have students practice pronouncing the past tense of these verbs, first as a class, then with a partner.

Link to *NorthStar: Reading and Writing*

If students are using the companion text, you may want to have them practice the pronunciation of the regular past tense forms found in Section 4B, Exercise 1 of that text.

✪✪✪ B   **STYLE: Expressing Agreement**

Suggested Time: 20 minutes ⏱

Focus

To help students express agreement in a conversation with *too* and *not . . . either*.

Setup

Read the material in the box aloud to the class. Have pairs (who are sitting next to each other) work on the exercise.

Expansion/Homework

You may want to try fluency lines (see page viii) with the students.

✪✪ C   **GRAMMAR: Simple Past Tense**

Suggested Time: 25 minutes ⏱

Focus

To have students practice using the simple past tense in the context of community gardens.

Setup

In Exercise 1, have students read the examples, then answer the questions about the verbs. Then ask them to read the grammar box silently. For Exercise 2, students can complete the exercise with the help of a dictionary and then check their answers with a partner. Practice reading aloud, taking turns with the two roles. Help with any pronunciation problems, paying particular attention to the pronunciation of the past tense marker *-ed*. Then, to do Exercise 3, pair students (of different fluency levels). Have students complete the first part of Exercise 4 on their own; then have them complete the chart in groups of four.

Expansion/Homework
(1) Assign Exercises 2 and 4 as homework. (2) For Exercise 3, have students write a time line for their own lives, then show the time line to a partner who asks questions. (3) For further practice, offer exercises from *Focus on Grammar, Basic* and from *Basic English Grammar*. See the Grammar Book References on page 167 of the Student Book for specific units and chapters.

Link to *NorthStar: Reading and Writing*
If students are using the companion text, ask them to discuss their answers to the questions in Section 4B, Exercise 3, in small groups. Ask them to pay particular attention to the pronunciation of the *-ed* endings while discussing their answers.

 For extra listening practice, have students use the NorthStar Companion Video.

✪✪✪ D SPEAKING TOPICS

Suggested Time: 20–25 minutes 🕐

Focus
To extend students' ability to talk about a place they know well; to talk extensively using the past tense.

Setup
Have students read the directions. Give students a few minutes to think about a place they have gone to enjoy nature and then answer the questions. Then have them work with a partner (of different fluency levels) to talk about the places they visited, perhaps showing pictures of them and answering any questions. Finally, have students tell the class about their partner's place.

Expansion/Homework
(1) You may want to ask students to add additional questions before completing the exercise. (2) These conversations could be in small groups. Encourage students in the group to acknowledge their similarities or differences as the speaker is explaining his place. For example, "Oh, I like beaches too."

Link to *NorthStar: Reading and Writing*
If students are using the companion text, you may want to have them write about the place they talked about, using Section 4B, Exercise 2, of the reading/writing text as a model.

✪ E RESEARCH TOPIC

Suggested Time: 30–50 minutes in class, 1–2 hours outside 🕐

Focus
To have students go outside the classroom to observe the green areas in their city or town, then report on what they see.

Setup
Brainstorm with students about places they could observe. List these on the board, and assign groups to different places/areas. Have students go out, observe an area, and answer the questions. Then they can present the information to the class in a report. While listening to their classmates' reports, students complete the chart. After each group has finished, discuss as a class.

Expansion/Homework
After students have reported to the class, you may want to have pairs of students tell each other about what they saw. The listener can ask questions and express agreement/disagreement based on personal experience.

Link to *NorthStar: Reading and Writing*
If students are also using the companion text, you may want to have them write a paragraph summarizing what they observed.

A Penny Saved Is a Penny Earned

OVERVIEW

Theme:	Money
Listenings:	Listening One: *A Barter Network* (a community meeting) Listening Two: *Saving Money* (three conversations)
Critical Thinking Skills:	Interpret a cartoon Assess personal consumer habits Interpret a time-line on the history of money Compare and contrast money and bartering systems Infer word meaning from context Identify advantages and disadvantages Evaluate consumer behavior
Listening Tasks:	Listen and predict Listen for main ideas Listen and take notes on details using an outline Interpret speaker's tone and emotions Relate listening to personal experiences Listen and take notes using a chart Summarize information from the two listenings Listen to and take notes on student reports
Speaking Tasks:	Make predictions Share opinions and experiences Role-play a group negotiation Make suggestions and come to an agreement Compare products Act out scripted conversations Ask and answer questions Simulate bartering Report on comparison shopping research
Pronunciation:	Numbers and prices
Vocabulary:	Context clues Word definitions
Grammar:	Comparative adjectives

UNIT SUMMARY

This unit deals with money: how to spend less of it. Listening One is a meeting about a bartering network. Listening Two includes three short informal conversations between friends about ways to save money.

The companion unit of *NorthStar: Reading and Writing* deals with counterfeit money and how new technologies have made it easier to counterfeit.

1 Focus on the Topic, PAGE 37

✪✪✪ A | PREDICTING

Suggested Time: 10 minutes ⏱

Focus
To get students thinking in general about saving money.

Setup
After students study the picture and the title, have them think about the questions before discussing their answers. As students answer the questions, write their ideas on the board to encourage all to participate.

Expansion/Homework
Have students work in pairs or share answers in small groups, then report their ideas to the class.

✪✪ B | SHARING INFORMATION

Suggested Time: 20 minutes ⏱

Focus
To get students thinking specifically about how they spend money in their own lives.

Setup
Have students mark their answers for Exercise 1 on their own, and then have them discuss in groups the questions in Exercise 2.

Expansion/Homework
(1) Have students discuss the questions as a class. (2) Ask students to discuss what the trends are in their own countries. What form of payment do most people use in their country? What form of payment do most people use in the rich countries of the world? In the poor countries of the world?

✪✪✪ C   PREPARING TO LISTEN

BACKGROUND
Suggested Time: 15 minutes ⏱

Focus
To learn a little about the history of money and introduce the concept of bartering.

Setup
Have students read the timeline and the questions that follow. Discuss as a class. Have students read the paragraph and work in pairs to discuss their answers, then share what they have talked about with the class. You may want to pair students up to encourage diversity of opinion (a male and a female student, a younger and an older student, or two students from different cultural backgrounds).

Expansion/Homework
You may ask students to complete this section at home, then discuss it in class.

VOCABULARY FOR COMPREHENSION
Suggested Time: 15 minutes ⏱

Focus
To introduce vocabulary and concepts related to money in preparation for the listening.

Setup
Have students complete the exercise individually; then go over answers as a class.

Expansion/Homework
Discuss the vocabulary in the context of students' everyday lives. For example: *How do you save money? What do you spend money on?*

2 Focus on Listening, PAGE 40

✪✪✪ A   LISTENING ONE: *A Barter Network*
Suggested Time: 10 minutes ⏱

Focus
To establish the context and tone of the listening text; to introduce the speaker; to predict what the segment will be about (joining a bartering network).

Setup

Have students listen to the segment, then answer the questions. Students can compare answers with those of a partner or share answers as a class. Note that there may be more than one answer to questions 3 and 4.

✪✪✪ LISTENING FOR MAIN IDEAS
Suggested Time: 10 minutes ⏱

Focus
To help students listen for the main ideas in the bartering exchange meeting.

Setup
Have the students read the statements, then mark them True or False. To help concentration, invite students to close their eyes during some of the listening. Have students compare their answers to those of a partner, then check them as a class.

Expansion/Homework
Have student listen again and rewrite each false sentence to make it true.

✪✪✪ LISTENING FOR DETAILS
Suggested Time: 15 minutes ⏱

Focus
To get students to listen carefully to the meeting again, this time for specific information.

Setup
First, have students fill in the information they already know. Then play the interview again. Have students fill in the rest of the missing information, then go over it as a class. If disagreements arise, replay the segment rather than simply giving the answer. Ask students if their predictions for the reading were correct.

Expansion/Homework
Before students complete the exercise, encourage them to retell the content of the listening piece. When you feel they understand the main ideas well enough, have them open their books and complete the exercise.

✪✪ REACTING TO THE LISTENING
Suggested Time: 20 minutes ⏱

Focus
To encourage students to make inferences based on tone of voice and word choice; to encourage students to listen beyond the literal meaning of the words.

Setup

To prepare students, have them read the questions for Excerpt One. Then play the excerpt and elicit several possible answers to the questions. Probe for reasons for students' choices. Help students focus on how the people speak rather than simply on what they say. Then continue with Excerpts Two and Three. Discuss the questions from Exercise 2 with the class.

Expansion/Homework

(1) In small groups, discuss question 1 of Exercise 2. (2) Imagine your group is a bartering exchange, discuss what services you could barter with each other. What skills does each member of the group have that could be used by other members, such as typing essays, cooking meals, or cleaning?

✪✪✪ B | LISTENING TWO: *Saving Money*

Suggested Time: 10 minutes ⏱

Focus

To get students thinking about ways to save money; to listen to informal conversation.

Setup

Ask students to look at the pictures and read the chart before you play the tape. After students have answered the questions, invite them to check their answers in pairs. Walk around the room and assist as needed. Play the tape again so students can complete the chart.

Expansion/Homework

You may want to have students listen to the tape and then answer the questions as a class.

✪✪✪ C | LINKING LISTENINGS ONE AND TWO

Suggested Time: 15 minutes ⏱

Focus

To get students to express opinions about money and saving.

Setup

Ask students to think about how they would answer the questions. Then divide the class into small groups (of different cultural backgrounds, if possible) to discuss their answers. Then the small groups can report the highlights of the discussion to the class, which you can note on the board.

Expansion/Homework

(1) Work with the whole class, getting students to listen and respond to one another's ideas. Encourage the use of vocabulary from Section 1C by listing it on the board and referring students to it. Correct pronunciation and usage errors orally and on the board. (2) You may want to have groups of students prepare thoughts for homework, then report to the class and discuss their opinions.

Link to *NorthStar: Reading and Writing*
If students are also using the companion text, you may ask them to consider these questions as well: *Counterfeiters try to copy real bills because they want to have more money to spend. People save money today so they will have more money to spend tomorrow. What are the advantages of counterfeiting over saving? What are the advantages of saving over counterfeiting?*

3 Focus on Vocabulary, PAGE 44

✪ EXERCISE 1
Suggested Time: 10 minutes

Focus
To work with unit vocabulary in context, first by supplying synonyms, then by using these new words in controlled conversation.

Setup
Have students complete the dialog on their own. Then have them work in pairs to practice the dialog: one student is A, the other student is B. They can practice until student B is comfortable enough with the lines to say them without using the text. The pairs then switch roles.

Expansion/Homework
(1) Have students do the exercise as homework, then practice in class. (2) Have students role play the conversation, paying attention to stress and intonation as they speak. (3) You may want to divide the class into two groups: one half reads the part of A, the other half reads the part of B.

✪ EXERCISE 2
Suggested Time: 15 minutes

Focus
To have students use the unit vocabulary in oral conversation.

Setup
Have students work in small groups to use new vocabulary in discussion. You can circulate to correct usage and pronunciation errors.

Expansion/Homework
Have students choose four of these questions to write answers for homework. They can share their answers with a classmate.

 For extra vocabulary practice, have students work on the self-grading vocabulary activities for the unit on the NorthStar Companion Website at **http://www.longman.com/northstar**.

4 Focus on Speaking, PAGE 46

✪✪A   PRONUNCIATION: Numbers And Prices

Suggested Time: 20 minutes 🕒

Focus
To develop awareness of syllable stress; to practice appropriate syllable stress using numbers and prices.

Setup
Have students listen to the examples given. Then have students listen to the tape and complete Exercise 1. Students can show what they have marked to a partner before listening again. For Exercise 2, have students work in pairs. Circulate as necessary to help with pronunciation and appropriate stress. Have students listen to the tape again for Exercise 3. Have students work in pairs (of the same gender, if possible) for Exercise 4.

Expansion/Homework
After students complete Exercise 2, write a list of prices on the board. Then have students practice pronouncing the number words with appropriate stress, first as a class, then individually. This can also be done for Exercise 3.

✪✪✪B   STYLE: Negotiating—Making Suggestions and Coming to an Agreement

Suggested Time: 20 minutes 🕒

Focus
To help students practice using simple negotiating language.

Setup
Read the introductory statement and the phrases in the box aloud to the class. Have students work on Exercise 1 on their own. For Exercise 2, put students in small groups and ask them to take turns suggesting things to buy. Everyone states their opinion about each item using the negotiating language. The group makes a final list of all the items they all agreed to buy. Finally, have the groups share their lists with other groups and discuss the differences and similarities in the lists.

Expansion/Homework
If you have access to a tape recorder, record some of the group conversations, then transcribe them for an error-correction exercise (see page vii).

✪✪C   GRAMMAR: Comparative Adjectives

Suggested Time: 25 minutes 🕒

Focus
To have students practice using comparative adjectives to discuss items to buy.

Setup

In Exercise 1, have students read the examples and answer the questions, then read the grammar box silently. Answer any questions that may arise. For Exercise 2, have students work in pairs. Have two students read the example so that the task is clear; they have to take turns comparing the two cars, using the adjectives provided. Walk around and cue students to correct their own errors in grammar, vocabulary, and pronunciation. For Exercise 3, students write their own sentences. You can correct them on the spot, and then students can read them aloud.

Expansion/Homework

(1) For Exercise 2, you may want to bring in car ads from magazines for students to compare. Or have students bring in ads. Or bring in advertisements for other items that have differences in size and price, for example, refrigerators, sofas, dresses. (2) For Exercise 2, students can write sentences with a partner or in small groups or work together as a class. (3) For further practice, offer exercises from *Focus on Grammar, Basic* and from *Basic English Grammar*. See the Grammar Book References on page 167 of the Student Book for specific units and chapters.

Link to *NorthStar: Reading and Writing*

If students are also using the companion text, you can ask them to use the transition words of addition and contrast that they studied in Section 4A when they write their sentences comparing the Pee Wee to the Indulge.

 For extra listening practice, have students use the NorthStar Companion Video.

✪✪✪ D   SPEAKING TOPICS

Suggested Time: 25–30 minutes

Focus

To develop students' ability to negotiate a bartering deal.

Setup

Provide each student with five note cards. Have students write on each of their cards the name of the item, how old it is, and how much it's worth. Students then walk around the classroom looking for good bartering exchanges following the model provided. Circulate among students to help them with ideas and language.

Expansion/Homework

You may want to video- or audiotape some of these bartering conversations. You can transcribe portions of them to use as an error-correction exercise. Or you can replay the tape, stopping it at key points and asking students to self-correct (see page vii).

✪E RESEARCH TOPIC

Suggested Time: 30–50 minutes in class, 1–2 hours outside 🕐

Focus
To get students to do comparison shopping for something they would like to buy.

Setup
Brainstorm with students about what they will go comparison shopping for and where. Students can complete their comparison shopping, then present their information to the class.

Expansion/Homework
(1) After students' presentations, you may want to have them discuss the types of stores they went to and how helpful the salesclerks were. (2) You may want to assign a paragraph in which students summarize their findings from the comparison shopping activity by answering these questions: *Where did you buy the item? Why?* (3) To expand on the unit's focus on money, you may want to send students to local banks to comparison shop for services such as checking and saving accounts.

Link to *NorthStar: Reading and Writing*
If students are also using the companion text, you may want to have them go to the bank and talk to a bank officer about counterfeit and authentic money. Students may want to ask questions such as: *What differences do you see? What features are bigger or smaller? How does the paper feel in comparison to real money?*

At Your Service: Service Animals

OVERVIEW	
Theme:	Animals
Listenings:	Listening One: *Kimba, the Hero Dog* (a news report)
	Listening Two: *Do People Help Animals Too?* (a conversation)
Critical Thinking Skills:	Interpret a bar graph
	Compare knowledge of service animals
	Infer word meaning from context
	Compare classmates' attitudes toward pets
	Interpret points of view
	Compare values about pets across cultures
	Evaluate appropriate language usage
Listening Tasks:	Listen and predict
	Listen and identify main ideas
	Listen for details
	Interpret speaker's tone and attitude
	Relate listening to personal values
	Listen to and comment on student reports
Speaking Tasks:	Make predictions
	Survey classmates
	Express opinions
	Construct and perform a dialogue
	Ask for more information
	Ask and answer information questions
	Conduct an interview
	Report interview results
Pronunciation:	Intonation of *wh*-questions
Vocabulary:	Context clues
	Word definitions
	Synonyms
	Appropriate word usage
Grammar:	Simple present tense—*wh*- questions with *do*

UNIT SUMMARY

This unit is about service animals (animals trained to assist people); what animals can do for people and what people can do to help animals. Listening One is a news report about a "hearing dog" who saved its owner from a fire. Listening Two is an informal conversation about how a dog trapped in a sewer pipe was rescued.

The companion unit of *NorthStar: Reading and Writing* deals with the problem of endangered animal species.

1 Focus on the Topic, PAGE 53

✪✪✪ A PREDICTING

Suggested Time: 10 minutes ⏱

Focus
To get students thinking about which animals Americans usually have as pets; to elicit ideas about how service animals are defined.

Setup
After students read the title and study the graph, have them think about the questions before discussing them as a class. As students answer the questions, write their answers on the board to encourage broad participation.

Expansion/Homework
(1) Have students work in pairs or share their answers in small groups, then report their ideas to the class. (2) You may want to ask students if these pets are common where they live.

Link to *NorthStar: Reading and Writing*
If students are using the companion text, you may want to have them look at the illustration in Section 1 of that text. Discuss the differences between domesticated (pets) and wild animals, extinct and living animals. Elicit examples.

✪✪ B SHARING INFORMATION

Suggested Time: 20 minutes ⏱

Focus
To discover students' interest in and experience with pets.

Setup

Divide the students into groups of four. Ask students to fill in the names of group members in the chart and write in answers during the discussion. Have one student summarize the group discussion for the class. Discuss the questions as a class.

Expansion/Homework

Have students write answers for themselves, then report to the group. One student per group can report to the class, tallying answers on the board. Lead a discussion about the class data.

✪✪✪ C   PREPARING TO LISTEN

BACKGROUND
Suggested Time: 15 minutes ⏱

Focus

To get students thinking of how animals might be of service to people.

Setup

Have students read the quiz and write their answers. Then have students read the paragraph on service animals. Answer any vocabulary questions. Discuss the questions as a class.

Expansion/Homework

(1) This can also be done for homework, followed by a class discussion.
(2) Working with the vocabulary lists, have students brainstorm other animals and other work that animals can do. Students should add these words and phrases to the lists. Students can then incorporate new words into the exercise.

VOCABULARY FOR COMPREHENSION
Suggested Time: 15 minutes ⏱

Focus

To introduce vocabulary and concepts related to service animals in preparation for the listening.

Setup

Have students read the paragraphs and complete the exercise individually, then pairs of students (of different fluency levels) can share their answers.

Expansion/Homework

(1) Assign as homework. Elicit answers and comments in class. (2) After students have completed the exercise, you may want to have them work in pairs to learn the vocabulary. One student can ask what a specific word in the reading means; his or her partner answers from the list of definitions. To add challenge, tell the student giving the definition not to look at the list.

✪✪✪ ❷ Focus on Listening, PAGE 56

✪✪✪ A   LISTENING ONE: *Kimba, the Hero Dog*

Suggested Time: 10 minutes ⏱

Focus
To establish the context and tone of the news report; to introduce the speakers; to elicit predictions about the content (fires and dogs, a special dog that helped someone, how dogs help people).

Setup
Have students read the questions, then listen to the first part of the segment and answer the questions. Students can read their answers to a partner or read them out loud to the class. Elicit several answers for question 3 and reasons for these choices.

✪✪✪ LISTENING FOR MAIN IDEAS

Suggested Time: 10 minutes ⏱

Focus
To help students listen for the main ideas of the news report about the heroic hearing dog, Kimba.

Setup
Have the students read the questions, then check the ones that are answered as they listen. To help concentration, invite students to close their eyes during some of the listening. Have students compare their answers to those of a partner, then check them as a class.

Expansion/Homework
(1) With books closed, you may want to have students listen to the segment once, then listen again for the questions. Then have them mark whether these questions were answered. (2) As a class, go over the answers to the questions. If there are any discrepancies, make a note on the board. Have students listen for this information when they listen again for details.

✪✪✪ LISTENING FOR DETAILS

Suggested Time: 15 minutes ⏱

Focus
To get students to listen carefully again, this time for specific information about how Kimba saved her owner.

Setup
First, have students read the sentences, marking the ones they already know. Play the news report again and let students compare their answers with those of a partner. If disagreements arise, replay the segment rather than simply giving the answer. Encourage students to give reasons for their answers.

Expansion/Homework

You may want to have students correct the false statements with a partner.

✪✪ REACTING TO THE LISTENING
Suggested Time: 15 minutes ⏱

Focus

To encourage students to make inferences based on tone of voice and word choice and to encourage students to share their own reactions to the material in the listening.

Setup

For Exercise 1, have students read the questions, then listen to Excerpt One. Elicit the answer to question 1, then elicit various answers to question 2. Focus students' attention on how tone of voice affects meaning in English. Then move on to Excerpt Two. Probe for reasons. For Exercise 2, give students time to read the excerpt and the questions. Then, discuss the questions as a class.

Expansion/Homework

Have students answer questions individually, then compare their answers with a partner's or share them with the class. Exercise 2 works well as a group discussion.

✪✪✪ B | LISTENING TWO: *Do People Help Animals, Too?*
Suggested Time: 15 minutes ⏱

Focus

To expand the theme by considering how people help animals; to introduce an informal conversation.

Setup

For Exercise 1, have students describe the picture as a class. Then ask them to look at the picture again and answer the questions in Exercise 2 in pairs (students who are sitting next to each other). Play the tape and invite students to check their answers. Walk around the room and assist as needed. In Exercise 4, get students to "listen between the lines" for people's feelings.

Expansion/Homework

You may want to have students listen to the tape once and then complete the exercises as a class. Write their answers on the board. They can listen to the tape again to confirm their answers.

Link to *NorthStar: Reading and Writing*

If students are using the companion text, you may want to have them discuss these questions: *The woman thought it was worth all the effort to save a single dog, Bandit. How much money would you spend to save the life of your pet? How much money should governments pay to save the lives of endangered animals in their country? Who should pay—the governments, local businesses, individual people?*

✪✪✪ C **LINKING LISTENINGS ONE AND TWO**

Suggested Time: 15 minutes ⏱

Focus

To get students to recall information and express opinions about animals and their relationship with people.

Setup

Divide the class into small groups (from different cultural backgrounds, if possible) to discuss their answers and complete the chart . Small groups can report the highlights of the discussion to the class, which you can note on the board.

Expansion/Homework

(1) Work with the whole class, getting students to listen and respond to one another's ideas. Encourage the use of vocabulary from Section 1 by listing it on the board and referring students to it. Correct pronunciation and usage errors orally and on the board. (2) You may want to have students prepare their answers for homework, then report to the class and discuss their opinions.

Link to *NorthStar: Reading and Writing*

If students are using the companion text, you may want to have them integrate ideas from Unit 4 into this discussion: *What animals are important in your culture? What animals are commonly used for service and what do they do? Are they well treated? Are any animals overworked or unprotected? How might we improve treatment of domesticated and wild animals?*

❸ Focus on Vocabulary, PAGE 60

✪ EXERCISE 1

Suggested Time: 10 minutes ⏱

Focus

To work with unit vocabulary in a conversational context.

Setup

Have students (of different fluency levels) work in pairs. One student reads the incorrect sentence. The listener corrects the sentence. Make sure students take turns being the reader and the checker.

Expansion/Homework

Assign as written homework. Students can check their answers with a partner in class.

✪ **EXERCISE 2**
Suggested Time: 15 minutes 🕐

Focus
To practice unit vocabulary in responding to conversation starters.

Setup
Have students work in pairs to complete this conversation. Circulate to help answer any questions and to correct any usage or pronunciation errors.

Expansion/Homework
Students can write sentences for homework. Have them share their sentences with a partner in class and practice saying the conversation.

Link to *NorthStar: Reading and Writing*
If students are also using the companion text, you may want to provide them with the vocabulary list from Unit 4 of both texts and ask them to write a short dialog about the endangered Thai elephants using this exercise as a model.

 For extra vocabulary practice, have students work on the self-grading vocabulary activities for the unit on the NorthStar Companion Website at **http://www.longman.com/northstar**.

4 Focus on Speaking, PAGE 62

✪✪ **A**   **PRONUNCIATION: Intonation of *Wh-* Questions**
Suggested Time: 15 minutes 🕐

Focus
To practice the intonation used with *wh-* questions in the context of the Kimba story.

Setup
Have students listen to the examples given. Then have students listen to Exercise 1 and complete the exercise. Students can compare their answers with those of a partner before listening again. For Exercise 2, have students work in pairs. Circulate as necessary to help with pronunciation and appropriate intonation.

Expansion/Homework
After students complete Exercise 2, have them brainstorm other *wh-* questions about the Kimba story, using the vocabulary in Section 1C. Write the questions on the board. Then have students practice asking and answering the questions with the appropriate intonation, first as a class, then individually.

Link to *NorthStar: Reading and Writing*

If students are also using the companion text, you may want to have them practice *wh-* questions with the vocabulary from Section 3 of that text. For example: *What do loggers do? What do poachers do? What does "extinct" mean? What does "endangered" mean?* and so on.

✪✪✪ B STYLE: Asking for More Information

Suggested Time: 20 minutes 🕐

Focus
To help students develop conversational skills by using follow-up questions.

Setup
Read the introductory statement and point out the follow-up questions that are underlined in Exercise 1. Then have pairs work on Exercises 1 and 2, using Exercise 2 as an opportunity to practice falling intonation with *wh-* questions.

Expansion/Homework
You may want to create a fluency line (see page viii).

Link to *NorthStar: Reading and Writing*
If students are using the companion text, you may want to have them identify the follow-up questions in Section 4B, Exercise 3, of that text.

✪✪ C GRAMMAR: Simple Present Tense—*Wh-* Questions With *Do*

Suggested Time: 25 minutes 🕐

Focus
To have students practice *wh-* questions in the simple present tense.

Setup
In Exercise 1, have students read the examples, then answer the questions. Next they can read the grammar box silently. Clear up any misunderstandings and then have students read the information on canine companions on their own. Answer any questions that come up about the concepts in this text. For Exercise 3, ask students (who are sitting next to each other) to work in pairs. Have two students read the example so that the roles are clear; one asks the question, the other answers. Walk around and cue students to correct their own errors in grammar, vocabulary, pronunciation, and intonation. Remind them to take turns asking and answering questions.

Expansion/Homework
(1) Bring in pictures involving animals and people for students to work with, for example, a farmer with animals, a professional dog walker, a veterinarian at work, and so on. It is important that pictures demonstrate people and animals at habitual/routine activities to establish a context for the appropriate use of the present tense. (2) You may want to have students practice asking *wh-* questions in small groups. The first student makes a sentence; the next uses that information as the basis for questions. For example, *She works in the circus*

every summer. Possible questions may include: *Why does she work at the circus? How often does she go to work? Where does she go in the winter?* The person who started with the sentence uses his or her imagination to answer. **(3)** For further practice, offer exercises from *Focus on Grammar, Basic* and from *Basic English Grammar.* See the Grammar Book References on page 167 of the Student Book for specific units and chapters.

Link to *NorthStar: Reading and Writing*
If students are using the companion text, have pairs of students write each other a letter following the guidelines in Section 4A of that text. The letter should be about a family pet, imagined or real, and some interesting story where the pet helped the family or the family helped the pet. In a follow-up letter, have students practice writing *Wh-* questions and follow-up questions about the first letter. Discuss any interesting or funny stories with the class.

For extra listening practice, have students use the NorthStar Companion Video.

✪✪✪D   SPEAKING TOPICS

Suggested Time: 30 minutes

Focus
To extend students' ability to ask questions and carry on a conversation in more sophisticated contexts.

Setup
Have students read the directions for Step 1, then divide them into groups, appointing a leader in each. Ask each group to choose which topic to discuss and then write the questions. You may want to do Topic 1 questions as a class to clarify the procedure. Then for Step 2, direct each group to discuss the topic, practicing follow-up questions. You should spend a few minutes listening in on each group to appreciate and facilitate the discussion. You may want to correct errors on the spot and, later, by using notes.

Expansion/Homework
(1) You may want to audio- or videotape conversations to use as an error-correction exercise. **(2)** You may want to have students use a nonverbal cue (such as a raised finger or pulling the ear lobe) with each other to indicate *wh-* questions that have been formed incorrectly. The student speaking should take this as a cue for self-correction.

Link to *NorthStar: Reading and Writing*
(1) If students are using the companion text, you may want to have them use the information they gather in Section 4D as the basis for another discussion. **(2)** Using the letter in Section 2A and the information about parts of a letter in Section 4A of that text, students can write letters to fellow students trying to convince them of their position on vegetarianism, the killing of animals for fur, or animal testing.

✪E RESEARCH TOPIC

Suggested Time: 30–50 minutes in class, 1–2 hours outside 🕐

Focus
To get students to ask people about their thoughts on service animals.

Setup
Brainstorm with students who they could interview. Have them role-play asking someone for an interview. You might want to give them some opening phrases such as: "Excuse me, could I ask you a few questions?" or "I'm doing an assignment for my English class. We've been talking about . . ." Ask students to conduct their interviews outside of class time. In class, have students present the information they found. While they are listening to their classmates' reports, encourage students to listen for similarities and differences in the opinions on the subject of service animals.

Expansion/Homework
After the classroom discussion, you may want to divide students into groups of three: one student (the speaker) gives his or her report, one student listens, and the third student takes notes. When the speaker finishes giving the report, the listener summarizes what he or she has said, and the note taker corrects the listener as necessary. Model good note-taking skills. Write some examples of notes on the board.

"Celletiquette"

OVERVIEW

Theme:	Cell Phone Etiquette
Listenings:	Listening One: *Everyone Has an Opinion* (a radio call-in show) Listening Two: *Our Listeners Write* (a radio call-in show)
Critical Thinking Skills:	Interpret a map and graphs Identify rationales for cell phone use Summarize and analyze student responses Infer information not explicit in text Infer word meaning from context Classify information Propose solutions Hypothesize reasons for cell phone behavior
Listening Tasks:	Listen and predict Listen and identify speakers' opinions Listen for supporting details Interpret speaker's tone and attitude Relate listening to personal etiquette standards Synthesize information from both listenings Listen to and comment on role-plays Listen to and take notes on students' reports
Speaking Tasks:	Make predictions Survey classmates Share opinions Compare and discuss solutions Use new vocabulary to talk about experiences Express likes and dislikes Interview classmates Role-play Report research findings
Pronunciation:	Unstressed *to*
Vocabulary:	Word definitions Context clues Appropriate word usage
Grammar:	Verbs plus gerunds and infinitives

UNIT SUMMARY

This unit is about cell phone use and abuse. Listening One is a call-in radio show where listeners call to tell the host what they like about cell phones and some of the problems they have with cell phones. Listening Two is the follow-up radio show where the hosts talks about some suggested solutions to rude cell phone behavior.

The companion unit of *NorthStar: Reading and Writing* deals with e-mail use and some of the problems associated with it.

1 Focus on the Topic, PAGE 69

✪✪✪ A PREDICTING

Suggested Time: 10 minutes ⏱

Focus
To get students thinking about cell phone use and who uses cell phones the most.

Setup
After students read the title and study the map, have them think about the questions before discussing them as a class. As students answer the questions, write their answers on the board to encourage broad participation.

Expansion/Homework
(1) Have students work in pairs or share their answers in small groups, then report their ideas to the class. (2) You may want to ask students about their own cell phone use. When did it start? Why?

Link to *NorthStar: Reading and Writing*
If students are using the companion text, you may want to have them look at the illustration in Section 1C of that text. Discuss the differences between total number of e-mail users and cell phone users worldwide. *Which technology is cheaper? Easier to gain access to? More useful? More reliable?*

✪✪ B SHARING INFORMATION

Suggested Time: 20 minutes ⏱

Focus
To discover students' interest in and experience with cell phones.

Setup
Divide the students into groups of four. Ask students to fill in the names of group members in the chart and write in answers during the discussion. Have one student summarize the group discussion for the class. Discuss the questions as a class, answering the questions listed in Exercise 3.

Expansion/Homework

Have students write answers for themselves, then report to the group. One student per group can report to the class, tallying answers on the board. Lead a discussion about the class data.

✪✪✪ C   PREPARING TO LISTEN

BACKGROUND
Suggested Time: 15 minutes ⏱

Focus

To get students thinking about why people use cell phones, and where using cell phones might be a problem.

Setup

Have students read the graphs and think about their answers to the questions. Then have students discuss their answers with a partner. Answer vocabulary questions (*banned* means "not allowed"). Discuss the questions as a class.

Expansion/Homework

(1) This can also be done for homework, followed by a class discussion.
(2) In small groups, have students discuss their own answers to these questions: *How necessary do you feel cell phones are in your life? Do you think cell phones should be banned in certain places? If so, where?*

VOCABULARY FOR COMPREHENSION
Suggested Time: 15 minutes ⏱

Focus

To introduce vocabulary and concepts related to cell phone use in preparation for the listening.

Setup

Have students work individually to read the statements and circle the correct definition. Then pairs of students (of different fluency levels) can share their answers. Discuss as a class and go over pronunciation.

Expansion/Homework

(1) Assign as homework. Elicit answers and comments in class. (2) After students have completed the exercise, you may want to have them work in pairs to learn the vocabulary. One student can ask what a specific word from the statements means; his or her partner provides the definition.

Link to *NorthStar: Reading and Writing*

If students are also using the companion text, you may want to provide them with a list of the vocabulary items from Section 1C from both texts. Ask them to look at the words from both texts and write down all the words that could be used to describe someone (adjectives) in one column and all the words that can be used to talk about what someone does (verbs) in another column.

② Focus on Listening, PAGE 73

✪✪✪ A LISTENING ONE: *Everyone Has an Opinion*
Suggested Time: 10 minutes ⏱

Focus
To establish the context and tone of the radio call-in show; to introduce the speakers; to elicit predictions about the content (cell phones, why people use them, and some problems they present).

Setup
Have students read the questions, then listen to the first part of the segment and answer the questions. Students can read their answers to a partner or read them out loud to the class. Elicit several answers for question 3 and reasons for these choices.

✪✪✪ LISTENING FOR MAIN IDEAS
Suggested Time: 10 minutes ⏱

Focus
To help students listen for the main ideas of the radio show about cell phones.

Setup
Have the students read the question and look at the chart. Make sure they understand the meanings of *pro* and *con*, then have them circle the right one as they listen. To help concentration, invite students to close their eyes during some of the listening. Have students compare their answers to those of a partner, then check them as a class.

Expansion/Homework
Ask students to make a short note about the caller's reaction to cell phones (for example: *Caller 4: pro safety*) next to each caller and discuss these as you go over the answers.

✪✪✪ LISTENING FOR DETAILS
Suggested Time: 15 minutes ⏱

Focus
To get students to listen carefully again, this time for specific information about what each caller said about cell phones.

Setup
First, have students read the choices, marking the ones they already know. Play the listening again and let students compare their answers with those of a partner. If disagreements arise, replay the segment rather than simply giving the answer. Encourage students to give reasons for their answers.

plete this exercise with a partner. (2) Have students
swers here to the notes they took if they did the
m Listening for Main Ideas. Were their notes accurate?

nts to make inferences based on tone of voice and word
lents share their own reactions to the material in the

ve students read the questions, then listen to the excerpts.
to question 1, then elicit various answers to question 2. Focus
on how tone of voice affects meaning in English. For Exercise
time to read the questions and mark their answers. Then have
the questions in small groups.

nework
e 1, answer questions as a class. (2) Have students mark their
xercise 2 at home and be prepared to discuss their answers in class.

ur Listeners Write

Suggested Time: ~~..~~ utes 🕐

Focus
To expand the theme by listening to talk-show listeners' suggestions on how to stop rude cell phone behavior.

Setup
Play the tape and invite students to circle the answer that best completes the sentences. Walk around the room and assist as needed.

Expansion/Homework
You may want to have students listen to the tape once and then complete the exercises as a class. Write their answers on the board. They can listen to the tape again to confirm their answers.

✪✪✪ C   LINKING LISTENINGS ONE AND TWO

Suggested Time: 15 minutes 🕐

Focus
To get students to recall information and express opinions about rude cell phone behavior.

Setup
First ask students to complete the chart on their own. Then divide the class into small groups (with students from different cultural backgrounds, if possible) to discuss their answers. Small groups can report the highlights of the discussion to the class, which you can note on the board.

Expansion/Homework
(1) Work with the whole class, getting students to listen and respond to one another's ideas. Encourage the use of vocabulary from Section 1 by listing it on the board and referring students to it. Correct pronunciation and usage errors orally and on the board. (2) You may want to have students prepare their answers for homework, then report to the class and discuss their opinions.

Link to *NorthStar: Reading and Writing*
If students are using the companion text, you may want to have them integrate ideas from Unit 5 into this discussion. For example, you could ask them to make a similar chart for e-mail use. In one column have them write some common problems with e-mail. In the second column have them write possible solutions. Are there any problems with solutions similar to those for cell phone use?

❸ Focus on Vocabulary, PAGE 77

✪ EXERCISE 1
Suggested Time: 20 minutes ⏱

Focus
To work with unit vocabulary in solving a crossword puzzle.

Setup
Have students (of different fluency levels) work in pairs. Student A reads his or her clues (across) to Student B. Student B first says his or her guess. Student A tells Student B if the guess is correct or incorrect. If B's guess is incorrect, A gives the correct answer. Student B writes the correct answer in place in the crossword puzzle. When B is finished, B gives A his or her clues (down).

Expansion/Homework
Ask the clue-giver to provide a sentence using the word in context for the guesser. You can circulate to help with this and make sure clue-givers are using correct pronunciation.

✪ EXERCISE 2
Suggested Time: 15 minutes ⏱

Focus
To practice unit vocabulary in asking and answering questions.

Setup
Have students work in small groups taking turns asking and answering the questions. Circulate to help answer any questions and to correct any usage or pronunciation errors.

Expansion/Homework
Students can write answers to these questions for homework. Have them share their answers with a partner in class and practice saying the dialogs.

Link to *NorthStar: Reading and Writing*
If students are also using the companion text, you may want to provide them with the vocabulary list from Unit 5 of both texts and ask them to include these questions when completing Exercise 2: *What kinds of things do you do to feel <u>calm</u>? Describe a time when you got <u>upset</u>? What happened to make you feel this way? What is your favorite <u>subject</u> to talk about with friends?*

For extra vocabulary practice, have students work on the self-grading vocabulary activities for the unit on the NorthStar Companion Website at **http://www.longman.com/northstar**.

4 Focus on Speaking, PAGE 79

 A | **PRONUNCIATION: Unstressed *to***

Suggested Time: 15 minutes

Focus
To practice speaking with the unstressed *to*.

Setup
Have students listen to the examples given. Then have students listen to Exercise 1 and repeat the lines. Then have students practice saying the chant with a partner. For Exercise 2, have students work in pairs to check the correct boxes. Then have the students take turns saying the sentences. Circulate as necessary to help with pronunciation and appropriate stress.

B | **STYLE: Expressing Likes and Dislikes**

Suggested Time: 20 minutes

Focus
To help students develop conversational skills by expressing likes and dislikes.

Setup

Read the introductory statements about expressing likes and dislikes. Add any additional ones that might arise in the discussion. Divide the class into two fluency lines, each line facing the other. Students stand directly across from their partner in the opposing line to ask and answer the questions. You can walk up and down the line spot-checking for errors. Encourage students to add the appropriate nonverbal cues that usually associate strong statements such as *It's great* or *I hate it.*

Expansion/Homework

This could also be set up as a partner exercise.

Link to *NorthStar: Reading and Writing*

If students are also using the companion text, you may want to have them write a partner five questions about e-mail modeled on these questions about cell phone use (for example: *How do you like e-mail?*). Have students exchange papers with their partner and then use these phrases to write answers. Ask students to pay special attention to the punctuation (Section 4A of the reading/writing text) of the likes and dislikes phrases.

✪✪ C   GRAMMAR: Verbs Plus Gerunds and Infinitives

Suggested Time: 25 minutes 🔊

Focus

To have students practice using gerunds and infinitives correctly in spoken discourse.

Setup

In Exercise 1, have students read the examples, then answer the questions. Next they can read the grammar box silently. Clear up any misunderstandings and then have students work in groups of three to complete the sentences in Exercise 2. Go over any difficult ones as a class. For Exercise 3, ask students to first choose the questions they want to ask and write them in the chart. Then give students time to talk to three different classmates and record their answers. Walk around and cue students to correct their own errors in grammar, vocabulary, pronunciation, and intonation. Discuss answers as a class.

Expansion/Homework

(1) Have students write four or five sentences describing what people need to do to have good "celletiquette." For example, people need to use a hands-free device when talking on the phone in the car. Have students check their sentences with a partner for any verb plus gerund and infinitive errors. (2) In pairs, have students tell each other what they like and dislike about cell phones. Have them listen carefully, checking for errors with gerunds and infinitives. (3) For further practice, offer exercises from *Focus on Grammar, Basic* and from *Basic English Grammar.* See the Grammar Book References on page 167 of the Student Book for specific units and chapters.

Link to *NorthStar: Reading and Writing*

If students are also using the companion text, have them discuss in small groups the following questions: *Cell phones and e-mail are both new technologies that have become extremely popular in the last five years. Discuss other new technologies that have developed in your lifetime. In general, do you like new technological tools or do you dislike them? Explain your answer.* Then ask students to write a short paragraph on that subject for homework.

 For extra listening practice, have students use the NorthStar Companion Video.

✪✪✪ D   SPEAKING TOPICS

Suggested Time: 30 minutes ⏱

Focus

To extend students' ability to carry on a conversation expressing likes and dislikes.

Setup

Have students read the directions for this section, then divide them into pairs and have them practice the example role-play. Then give students time to write out and practice the role-play they chose. Have each pair perform their role-play before the class. Discuss them all after each pair has performed. You may want to correct errors on the spot and, later, by using notes.

Expansion/Homework

You may want to audio- or videotape role plays to use as an error-correction exercise.

Link to *NorthStar: Reading and Writing*

If students are also using the companion text, you may want to have them discuss Topics 2 and 4 from Section 4C in small groups. Encourage students to use vocabulary from both units when discussing these topics and to pay close attention to their gerund and infinitive use with verbs.

✪ E   RESEARCH TOPIC

Suggested Time: 30–50 minutes in class, 1–2 hours outside 🕐

Focus

To get students to talk to people out in the world about other high-tech communication devices.

Setup

Brainstorm with students additional high-tech communication devices as well as local vendors of these items. Have them role-play asking someone a few questions. You might want to give them some opening phrases such as: "Excuse me, could I ask you a few questions?" or "I'm doing an assignment for my English class. We've been talking about . . . ." Send students out to get the information requested. In class, have students present information on the device they chose. While they are listening to their classmates' reports, encourage students to listen for which device they would most want to buy.

Expansion/Homework

You might ask students to write up the results of their research for homework.

Link to *NorthStar: Reading and Writing*

Refer students to Unit 3, Section 4A, of the reading/writing text to review transition words of addition and contrast. Have students write a paragraph discussing what's good and what's bad about cell phones. They can draw on material presented in the listening, their research in Section 4E, or their own experience.

Is It Women's Work?

OVERVIEW

Theme:	Male and Female Roles
Listenings:	Listening One: *Who's Taking Care of the Children?* (a TV talk show) Listening Two: *Who Is Right for the Job?* (three conversations)
Critical Thinking Skills:	Identify assumptions about family roles Interpret a graph and a chart Identify personal assumptions Infer word meaning from context Rank child-care solutions Support opinions with reasoning Compare gender roles across cultures
Listening Tasks:	Listen and predict Listen and identify chronology in a text Listen for details Interpret speaker's tone and attitude Listen and take notes using a chart Relate listenings to personal values Synthesize information from both listenings Listen to and comment on student reports
Speaking Tasks:	Make predictions Survey classmates Express opinions Act out scripted conversations Use new vocabulary in open conversation Use intonation to denote attitude Agree and disagree Ask and answer questions about daily habits Report on observation of gender roles
Pronunciation:	Rising and falling intonation patterns
Vocabulary:	Context clues Word definitions Idiomatic expressions
Grammar:	Adverbs and expressions of frequency

UNIT SUMMARY

This unit deals with gender stereotypes and work. Listening One features a television talk-show interview of a male nanny. Listening Two involves three short, informal conversations about men and women in jobs that are unusual for their gender.

The companion unit of *NorthStar: Reading and Writing* deals with household chores and who typically does them.

1 Focus on the Topic, PAGE 85

✪✪✪A PREDICTING

Suggested Time: 10 minutes ⏱

Focus
To get students thinking about the division of labor in the home.

Setup
After students look at the picture and the title, have them think about the questions before discussing them as a class. As students answer the questions, write their answers on the board to encourage participation and use of new vocabulary.

Expansion/Homework
Have students work in pairs or share answers in small groups, then report their ideas to the class.

Link to *NorthStar: Reading and Writing*
If students are using the companion text, you may want to integrate ideas from Section 1A in this discussion. Ask: *According to the ads on page 101, how did women feel about housework in the 1950s?*

✪✪B SHARING INFORMATION

Suggested Time: 15 minutes ⏱

Focus
To find out who does household chores in the students' homes.

Setup
Divide the class into groups of four. Have them read the directions. Then have students fill in the names of group members in the chart and write down the responses. Afterwards, have them discuss the answers.

Expansion/Homework
(1) You may want to have each student write down his or her responses first, then tell the group. (2) You may want to have one student from each group report to the class, using the four questions to organize the information.

✪✪✪ C   PREPARING TO LISTEN

BACKGROUND
Suggested Time: 15 minutes ⏱

Focus
To get students thinking about work and gender, which gender tends to do which kind of work.

Setup
Have students read the information and graph. Answer any vocabulary questions. Have students work in pairs, answering the questions in Exercise 2. To encourage a lively discussion, mix men and women, older and younger students, students from differing cultural backgrounds, and so on. Move among the pairs, listening in, making corrections, and offering encouragement.

Expansion/Homework
(1) These exercises can also be done for homework, with class discussion following. (2) Also, Exercise 2 works well with students in groups of three or four.

VOCABULARY FOR COMPREHENSION
Suggested Time: 15 minutes ⏱

Focus
To introduce vocabulary and concepts related to childcare in preparation for the listening.

Setup
Have students read the paragraphs and complete the exercise individually. Then have them compare their answers with a partner (from a different language background, if possible).

Expansion/Homework
(1) You may want to assign this exercise for homework, then check it in class, working on pronunciation, too. (2) After students have completed the exercise, you may want to have them work in pairs to learn the vocabulary. Student A can ask what a specific word in the reading means; Student B answers from the list of definitions. To add challenge, tell Student B not to look at the list.

Link to *NorthStar: Reading and Writing*
If students are also using the companion text, provide them with a list of words from this text and ask them as a class to make a list of household chores that a typical family in their community would do on a daily basis. Have them compare lists with students from other countries. How different or similar are the lists?

2 Focus on Listening, PAGE 88

✪✪✪ A   LISTENING ONE: *Who's Taking Care of the Children?*
Suggested Time: 15 minutes 🕐

Focus
To establish the context and tone of a television talk show; to introduce the speaker; to elicit predictions about the questions the interviewer will ask.

Setup
Ask students to read the questions, then listen to the first part of the segment and answer the questions. Students can read their answers to a partner or to the class. Put prediction questions on the board for later reference.

✪✪✪ LISTENING FOR MAIN IDEAS
Suggested Time: 15 minutes 🕐

Focus
To help students listen for the main ideas in the interview with a male nanny.

Setup
Have the students read the list of issues, then order them as they listen. To help concentration, invite students to close their eyes during the listening. Have students compare their answers to those of a partner, then check them as a class.

Expansion/Homework
You may want to have students complete this activity as a class.

✪✪✪ LISTENING FOR DETAILS
Suggested Time: 15 minutes 🕐

Focus
To get students to listen again, this time for specific information.

Setup
First, have students read the sentences, circling the answers they already know. Play the interview again, then have students compare their answers to those of a partner. If disagreements arise, replay the segment rather than simply giving the answer. Have students look at the prediction questions from Section 2A (on the board) and discuss.

Expansion/Homework
If students have a strong reaction to the idea of a male nanny, you might want to encourage them to express their views at this point in a brief discussion.

✪✪ REACTING TO THE LISTENING
Suggested Time: 15 minutes 🕐

Focus
To encourage students to make inferences based on tone of voice and word choice; to encourage students to listen beyond the literal meaning of the words.

Setup
For Exercise 1, have students read the questions, then listen to Excerpt One. Discuss the questions as a class. Ask students to listen for the tone of voice and notice how it affects meaning. Have students do Excerpts Two and Three on their own. Discuss as a class. For Exercise 2, give students time to read and think about their answers. Discuss answers as a class.

Expansion/Homework
Exercise 2 could be done in small groups with highlights of the discussion shared with the whole class.

Link to *NorthStar: Reading and Writing*
If students are also using the companion book, have them look again at Exercise 1 in Section 2A, Reacting to the Reading. Have students rewrite items 2, 3, 5, 6, and 7 from the list of statements replacing the word *housework* with the word *childcare*. In small groups, have students decide if they agree or disagree with this statement and why. Highlights of this discussion should be shared with the class.

✪✪✪ B LISTENING TWO: *Who Is Right for the Job?*
Suggested Time: 15 minutes 🕐

Focus
To add examples of gender stereotypes and work; to expose students to informal conversations to contrast with Listening One.

Setup
For Exercise 1, have students match the conversation to the job title while listening to the tape. For Exercise 2, ask students to read the chart and complete it while listening to the tape. Invite students to check their answers in pairs. Walk around the room and assist as needed.

Expansion/Homework
You may want to have students listen to the tape once, then complete the exercises as a class. Write their answers on the board. Leave blanks and put question marks to indicate missing or incorrect/incomplete information. They can listen to the tape again to confirm their answers.

✪✪✪C LINKING LISTENINGS ONE AND TWO

Suggested Time: 15 minutes ⏱

Focus

To get students to express their own opinions regarding the jobs and gender stereotypes discussed in the unit.

Setup

Have students write down and then discuss their answers with the class.

Expansion/Homework

(1) Encourage the use of vocabulary from Sections 2A and 2B by listing it on the board and referring students to it. Correct pronunciation and usage errors orally and on the board. (2) You may want to have students prepare their answers for homework, then check answers with the class and discuss their opinions. (3) During the class discussion, ask students to note any cultural differences in how men and women are viewed. Ask students about traditional activities for men and women in their cultures. Have these traditional roles changed any since they were young? How? (4) You may want to have men and women work in separate groups to discuss these items. Then have each group share highlights of their discussion with the class.

Link to *NorthStar: Reading and Writing*

If students are also using the companion text, they learned that what was true for housework in the 1950s is not true in the 2000s. Have students consider and discuss in small groups the differences in childcare (who does it, how much time children spend in childcare, what children do in childcare) in their country from 1950 to 2000.

❸ Focus on Vocabulary, PAGE 91

✪ EXERCISE 1

Suggested Time: 10 minutes ⏱

Focus

To work with definitions and usage of unit vocabulary.

Setup

Have students work individually to complete the exercise and check answers with the class. Then, in pairs, have students practice the conversation, changing roles after item 4.

Expansion/Homework

Assign for homework and practice in class.

⊘ **EXERCISE 2**
Suggested Time: 15 minutes ⏱

Focus
To practice using unit vocabulary in casual conversations.

Setup
In small groups, have students take turns asking each other the questions. Everyone answers the questions. Have students correct each other on pronunciation and usage. Discussion highlights should be shared with the class.

Expansion/Homework
These questions could be written out for homework and exchanged with a partner in class. After the partner reads the answer, the partners ask questions and discuss the answers.

 For extra vocabulary practice, have students work on the self-grading vocabulary activities for the unit on the NorthStar Companion Website at **http://www.longman.com/northstar**.

4 Focus on Speaking, PAGE 93

✪✪ A   PRONUNCIATION: Intonation
Suggested Time: 20 minutes ⏱

Focus
To discover and recognize how intonation affects word meaning using the context of childcare.

Setup
Have students listen to the examples and discuss them. Then have students complete Exercise 1. Discuss answers as a class. Replay the tape to clarify. For Exercise 2, have students read the short exchanges, making the appropriate intonations as directed.

Expansion/Homework
You may want to refer students to the audioscript on page 169. Have students work in pairs to practice rising and falling intonation in the conversations.

Link to *NorthStar: Reading and Writing*
If students are also using the companion text, you may want to have them practice with some of the sentences from Section 3, Exercise 1. Have students read the sentences and circle those that would be most appropriate to work with. Then in pairs, one student says the sentence, the other responds with *Really, Well,* or *Hmm,* with intonation that conveys a specific intent.

✪✪✪B   STYLE: Expressing Opinions and Agreeing or Disagreeing

Suggested Time: 25 minutes 🕙

Focus
To give students language for and practice in expressing personal opinions.

Setup
Have students read the introductory statement and the examples, then work in groups of three to express and develop their opinions. Encourage them to support their opinions with examples. Elicit an example to show how.

Expansion/Homework
(1) You may want to have students prepare for the activity by writing down the reasons they will use to back up their opinions. (2) You may want to have students form a fluency line (see page viii).

✪✪C   GRAMMAR: Adverbs and Expressions of Frequency

Suggested Time: 30 minutes 🕙

Focus
To have students discover and practice appropriate use of frequency adverbs and related expressions.

Setup
In Exercise 1, have students read the examples, then answer the questions. Next, ask them to read the grammar box silently. For Exercise 2, invite students to stand up and walk around, asking questions and writing answers. Walk around and cue students to correct their own errors in grammar.

Expansion/Homework
(1) Write the frequency adverbs in a horizontal line across the board: *always/ usually/often/sometimes/rarely/never*. After students have finished writing sentences in Exercise 2, you may want to have them substitute a frequency adverb for the time expression in the sentence; for example, *Ming cleans his house once a week. Ming often cleans his house.* Correct word order. Call on students to read their new sentences out loud. (2) For further practice, offer exercises from *Focus on Grammar, Basic* and from *Basic English Grammar*. See the Grammar Book References on page 167 of the Student Book for specific units and chapters.

 For extra listening practice, have students use the NorthStar Companion Video.

✪✪✪D   SPEAKING TOPICS

Suggested Time: 25 minutes 🕙

Focus
To extend students' ability to ask questions and carry on a conversation about gender and work; to integrate ideas, vocabulary, and grammar into a higher-level task.

Setup

In small groups (from different cultural backgrounds, if possible), have students read the directions and then discuss the statements in the manner suggested in Step 2. Ask students to help each other with error correction. You should circulate to help with this as well.

Link to *NorthStar: Reading and Writing*

If students are also using the companion text, ask them to discuss in their groups Topic 2 in Section 4C from the reading/writing text.

✪E   RESEARCH TOPIC

Suggested Time: 30–50 minutes in class, 1–2 hours outside 🕐

Focus

To expand students' awareness of typical jobs for men and women in their area.

Setup

Brainstorm with students about where they could observe men and women at work. During the class discussion about what students observed, have classmates listen for what they think is the most unusual job that a man or woman was observed doing. Encourage students to give reasons (Section 4B) and use adverbs of frequency (Section 4C).

Expansion/Homework

(1) You may want to have students discuss what they observed in small groups. (2) You can ask students to interview friends or neighbors. At the next class session, they can share the highlights of those discussions. (3) You may want to have students write a paragraph about their observations, using vocabulary, grammar, and ideas from the unit.

Good-Mood Foods

OVERVIEW	
Theme:	Food
Listenings:	Listening One: *Would You Like to Be on the Radio?* (a radio show) Listening Two: *What's the Matter?* (four cases)
Critical Thinking Skills:	Identify personal attitudes toward food Interpret a chart Infer word meaning from context Categorize words and sounds Propose solutions Compare and contrast sounds Rank student findings
Listening Tasks:	Listen and predict Listen for main ideas Listen and identify details Interpret speaker's tone and reaction Relate listening to personal experiences Listen and take notes using a chart Integrate information from both listenings in discussion Listen to and comment on student reports and reviews
Speaking Tasks:	Make predictions Survey classmates Express opinions Compare and discuss solutions Politely express wants Role-play Discuss a shopping list Plan a dinner and report to class Present a restaurant review
Pronunciation:	Vowels [ʊ] and [uw]
Vocabulary:	Word definitions Synonyms Vocabulary classification Context clues Word association
Grammar:	Count and non-count nouns

UNIT SUMMARY

This unit focuses on the affect of food on mood. Listening One involves person-on-the-street interviews about food and moods. Listening Two includes three short personal statements revealing strong moods.

The companion unit of *NorthStar: Reading and Writing* deals with the advantages and disadvantages of organic foods.

1 Focus on the Topic, PAGE 99

✪✪✪A PREDICTING

Suggested Time: 10 minutes

Focus
To get students thinking about the food people choose and its relationship to their moods.

Setup
After students study the picture and the title, let them think about the questions before discussing their answers as a class. As students answer the questions, write their answers on the board to encourage participation and to supply vocabulary.

Expansion/Homework
(1) Have students work in pairs or share answers in small groups, then report their ideas to the class. (2) You may want to ask students what they eat when they are feeling sad.

✪✪B SHARING INFORMATION

Suggested Time: 10 minutes

Focus
To discover students' reasons for choosing the foods they eat.

Setup
Have students complete the exercises, then discuss their answers in small groups (of different cultural backgrounds, if possible).

Expansion/Homework
(1) Before students complete Exercise 1, you may want to have them brainstorm other issues that are important to them in choosing what they eat. Students can then include these items in the list for ranking. (2) After students have finished Exercise 2, you may want to have one student summarize the group discussion for the class.

✪✪✪C PREPARING TO LISTEN

BACKGROUND
Suggested Time: 10 minutes ⏱

Focus
Use the food pyramid to get students to analyze the nutritional value of some food items.

Setup
Have students read the introductory paragraph and complete the exercises in pairs. Answer any vocabulary questions. Have students work with a partner (from a different language background, if possible).

Expansion/Homework
After Exercise 1, have students put food items they normally eat into the categories. Help with vocabulary.

VOCABULARY FOR COMPREHENSION
Suggested Time: 15 minutes ⏱

Focus
To introduce vocabulary that is related to moods and feelings in preparation for the listening.

Setup
Have students complete the exercises individually, then compare their answers with those of a partner.

Expansion/Homework
You may want to assign the exercises as homework, then have students read their answers aloud in class.

Link to *NorthStar: Reading and Writing*
If students are also using the companion text, ask them to work in pairs to write five minidialogs based on these words from the reading/writing text: *fresh, tastes, natural, produce, old-fashioned*. Have students use the dialogs in Exercise 1 as a model.

② Focus on Listening, PAGE 103

✪✪✪A LISTENING ONE: *Would You Like to Be on the Radio?*

Suggested Time: 10 minutes ⏱

Focus
To establish the context and tone of a person-on-the-street radio show; to introduce the speakers; to elicit predictions about the short interviews.

Setup

Have students read the questions, then listen to the first part of the segment and answer the questions. Have students read their answers out loud to the class.

✪✪✪ LISTENING FOR MAIN IDEAS
Suggested Time: 15 minutes ⏲

Focus
To help students listen for the main ideas of the radio interview.

Setup
Have the students read the sentences, then mark their answers as they listen. To help concentration, invite students to close their eyes during some of the listening. Have students compare their answers to those of a partner, then check them as a class.

Expansion/Homework
Have students correct the false sentences.

✪✪✪ LISTENING FOR DETAILS
Suggested Time: 15 minutes ⏲

Focus
To get students to listen again, this time for specific information.

Setup
First, have students read the chart, writing down the answers they already know. Play one radio interview and discuss answers. Then play the other two interviews and have students work in pairs to compare their answers. If disagreements arise, replay the segment rather than simply giving the answer. Have students look at their predictions from Section 2A and compare.

✪✪ REACTING TO THE LISTENING
Suggested Time: 15 minutes ⏲

Focus
To encourage students to make inferences based on tone of voice and word choice; to encourage students to listen beyond the literal meaning of the words.

Setup
For Exercise 1, have students read the questions for Excerpt One. Then play the excerpt and elicit the answers to the questions. Elicit several possible answers. Then do the same for Excerpt Two. Probe for reasons for students' choices. Get them to identify words and tone of voice. For Exercise 2, give students time to read the questions and think about their answers. Discuss as a class.

Expansion/Homework
(1) You may want to let pairs work together first, then discuss as a class.
(2) Exercise 2 could be assigned for written homework and discussed in class.

✪✪✪ B LISTENING TWO: *What's the Matter?*

Suggested Time: 15 minutes ⏰

Focus
To encourage students to think further about moods and food; to give practice listening to short, informal statements.

Setup
Have students look at the chart, then listen to the tape. Ask students to complete the chart and discuss their answers with the class.

Expansion/Homework
You may want to have students listen to the tape once and then work in pairs to complete the exercise. Write their answers on the board. They can listen to the tape again to confirm their answers.

✪✪✪ C LINKING LISTENINGS ONE AND TWO

Suggested Time: 10 minutes ⏰

Focus
To get students to express opinions about the relationship between food and moods; to encourage them to discuss other ways to change their moods.

Setup
Have pairs of students (of the same gender) prepare the answers to the questions. Then encourage students to discuss the questions as a class.

Expansion/Homework
(1) Work with the whole class, getting students to listen and respond to one another's ideas. Encourage the use of vocabulary from Sections 1C by listing it on the board and referring students to it. Correct pronunciation and usage errors orally and on the board. (2) You may want to have students prepare their answers for homework, then report to the class and discuss their opinions.

Link to *NorthStar: Reading and Writing*
If students are also using the companion text, you may want to have them integrate ideas from Unit 7 of that text in this discussion. Ask questions such as: *Are there any natural foods or products you use when you are in a good mood? a bad mood?*

3 Focus on Vocabulary, PAGE 106

✪ EXERCISE 1
Suggested Time: 15 minutes ⏰

Focus
To work with unit vocabulary (words, phrases, and verbs).

Setup
Have students work in pairs (sitting next to each other) to read the chart, then fill in words from the list given. They can then read their answers to the class.

Expansion/Homework
(1) After students have completed this exercise, you may want to have them work with a partner (of similar fluency) to learn the vocabulary. Pass out index cards to pairs of students. On each card have them write one word from the list (not including the verbs). Have one student hold the pile of cards and pull one out. The other student must make a sentence using the word along with the correct verb. (2) If time permits, have students work in pairs to write a conversation. Have them include all the words featured in Exercise 1. Circulate as necessary to correct; then have pairs practice the conversation aloud.

✪ EXERCISE 2
Suggested Time: 15 minutes

Focus
To create sentences using unit vocabulary.

Setup
Have each student in the class take a turn making a sentence using the words in the box. Then have classmates help correct any mistakes.

Expansion/Homework
(1) Have students create these sentences in pairs and share with the class.
(2) Assign this part for homework and have pairs of students exchange sentences in class to check for accuracy.

✪ EXERCISE 3
Suggested Time: 15 minutes

Focus
To have students practice speaking using the unit vocabulary.

Setup
Have students work in pairs taking turns asking and answering the questions.

Expansion/Homework
(1) Have students discuss these questions in small groups. (2) Assign questions 3 and 5 for homework.

 For extra vocabulary practice, have students work on the self-grading vocabulary activities for the unit on the NorthStar Companion Website at **http://www.longman.com/northstar**.

4 Focus on Speaking, PAGE 107

✪✪ A PRONUNCIATION: Vowels [ʊ] and [uw]

Suggested Time: 10 minutes ⏲

Focus
To discover and practice the pronunciations of the [ʊ] and [uw] vowel sounds.

Setup
Have students read the description and listen to the examples given, then listen and repeat the sentence in Exercise 1. For Exercise 2 have students listen to the tape and put the right word in the appropriate box. Then students can compare their answers with a partner and practice saying the words (Exercise 3). For Exercise 4, play the tape and have students individually mark the vowel sounds as S (same) or D (different). Discuss as a class. For Exercise 5, have students practice asking and answering the questions in pairs. Circulate as necessary to help.

Expansion/Homework
Have students brainstorm other words with the [ʊ] or [uw] vowel sound. Write them on the board. Then have students practice pronouncing these words, first as a class, then as individuals.

✪✪✪ B STYLE: Politely Expressing Wants

Suggested Time: 20 minutes ⏲

Focus
To help students learn the language for expressing and asking about wants.

Setup
Read the introductory statement and the examples in the chart to the class. Divide the students into pairs to work on Exercise 1. Have a pair read the conversation aloud. For Exercise 2, encourage students to have fun during the role play. The waiter can stand while the customer sits and waits expectantly.

Expansion/Homework
(1) Have some pairs perform for the class. You may want to give written feedback on pronunciation and grammar. (2) Have students bring in menus to work with from nearby restaurants. To extend the conversation in Exercise 2, the waiter can offer suggestions about what to eat and explain items on the menu.

✪✪ C GRAMMAR: Count and Non-Count Nouns

Suggested Time: 25 minutes ⏲

Focus
To have students recognize and produce the difference between count and non-count nouns; to point out related grammatical elements: *some* vs. *any*; presence or absence of the indefinite article; presence or absence of the plural -*s*; quantity words.

Setup
For Exercise 1, ask students to read the examples and answer the questions. Then have them read the grammar box silently. Students can work in pairs to do Exercises 2 and 3. You should listen in and correct. Encourage a playful atmosphere.

Expansion/Homework
(1) Have students brainstorm a list of food items that you write on the board (in their singular form). Then have them take a piece of paper and make two columns, one for count nouns, one for non-count nouns. Have them write the food items from the board in the appropriate column. Students can read answers to a partner or to the class. Then have students practice the conversation in Exercise 3, using food items from this list. Encourage students to work with singular and plural forms. (2) For further practice, offer exercises from *Focus on Grammar, Basic* and from *Basic English Grammar*. See the Grammar Book References on page 167 of the Student Book for specific units and chapters.

Link to *NorthStar: Reading and Writing*
Using listening/speaking Exercise 3 as a model, have students look at Section 4B, Exercise 4, in the reading/writing text and talk about what Alice does and doesn't need.

 For extra listening practice, have students use the NorthStar Companion Video.

✪✪✪ D SPEAKING TOPICS

Suggested Time: 20–25 minutes

Focus
To extend students' ability to ask questions about wants and carry on a conversation related to food.

Setup
Have students read the directions. Ask if they have any experience with potluck dinners. Divide students into groups of three to plan their parties. Circulate to help with any vocabulary needs that may arise. For Step 2, have one student report to the class.

Expansion/Homework
You may want to have a potluck dinner. Have students present their dishes by giving the name and the ingredients before setting them on the table.

Link to *NorthStar: Reading and Writing*
If students are also using the companion text, you may want to have them write down the recipe for their potluck dish, using the recipe on page 138 of the reading/writing text as a model.

⭐E   RESEARCH TOPIC

Suggested Time: 30–50 minutes in class, 1–2 hours outside 🕐

Focus
To get students to visit and evaluate restaurants in their community.

Setup
Brainstorm with students about where they could go to eat. Add your ideas. Form groups and assign a "restaurant day." Students can then report on local restaurants to the class.

Expansion/Homework
(1) You may want to have students review the school cafeteria if there is one.
(2) You may want to have students write restaurant reviews and compile them in a brochure about the neighborhood. For fun, they can rate each place with forks or stars: from one (fair) to three (excellent).

An Ice Place to Stay

OVERVIEW

Theme:	Travel
Listenings:	Listening One: *An Unusual Vacation* (a travel hotline) Listening Two: *Vacations Around the World* (three vacation packages)
Critical Thinking Skills:	Infer situational context Interpret a map Rank personal preferences in travel Categorize information Compare and contrast sounds Evaluate vacation places according to different criteria
Listening Tasks:	Listen and predict Listen for main ideas Listen and categorize details Interpret speaker's tone and attitude Relate listenings to personal interests Listen and take notes on student information Connect themes between two listenings Take dictation Talk to travel agents to research a vacation place
Speaking Tasks:	Make predictions Express opinions Make polite requests Role-play a conversation at an information desk Conduct an interview Agree and disagree Ask and answer travel questions Use new vocabulary in an open conversation Report research findings
Pronunciation:	*Can* and *can't*
Vocabulary:	Context clues Dictionary work Vocabulary classification
Grammar:	*Can* and *can't*

UNIT SUMMARY

This unit explores unusual vacation spots around the world, including a Swedish hotel made entirely of ice and snow. Listening One, a telephone conversation with a prospective guest and the Swedish tourist information hotline operator, describes the Ice Hotel in northern Sweden. Listening Two includes three descriptions of other vacation spots: in the United States, Nepal, and Indonesia.

The companion unit of *NorthStar: Reading and Writing* explores alternatives to air travel.

1 Focus on the Topic, PAGE 115

✪✪✪ A   PREDICTING

Suggested Time: 10 minutes

Focus
To get students thinking about the Ice Hotel; to introduce the context of the listening.

Setup
After students look at the picture and the title, ask them to think about the questions before discussing them as a class. As students answer the questions, write their answers on the board to encourage broad participation and use of appropriate vocabulary. Point out the word play in the title: "an ice" sounds the same as "a nice."

Expansion/Homework
(1) Have students work in pairs or share answers in small groups, then report their ideas to the class. (2) You may want to ask students if they know of any unusual places to stay.

Link to *NorthStar: Reading and Writing*
If students are also using the companion text, you may want to have them integrate ideas from the discussion in Section 1 of that text. Ask them where they think the Ice Hotel is and how they would get there.

✪✪ B   SHARING INFORMATION

Suggested Time: 10–15 minutes

Focus
To discover what is important to students in choosing a place to visit.

Setup

Have students read and then rank the items in the list. In small groups, invite them to discuss how important each item is and where they might find information for vacation planning (e.g., a travel agent, friends, the Internet). Then one student can summarize the group discussion for the class.

Expansion/Homework

(1) You may want to have students work in pairs to rank and discuss items. (2) You may want to list the top one or two items from each student and ask them to explain their choices to the class.

✪✪✪ C PREPARING TO LISTEN

BACKGROUND
Suggested Time: 15 minutes

Focus

To introduce information about Sweden: location, geography, and weather.

Setup

Have students work in small groups with a group leader. After they read silently, the leader can ask the questions.

Expansion/Homework

(1) You may want to have students complete this exercise as homework, then discuss in class. (2) To clarify Sweden's location, you could bring in a world map.

Link to *NorthStar: Reading and Writing*

If students are also using the companion text, you may want to have them research ways of traveling to Sweden after you have discussed Section 1B of that text.

VOCABULARY FOR COMPREHENSION
Suggested Time: 20 minutes

Focus

To introduce vocabulary and concepts related to tourism in preparation for the listening.

Setup

In Exercise 1, ask students to look up unfamiliar words in the dictionary, then discuss the meanings of those words in class. Students can then complete Exercises 2 and 3, checking their answers with a partner. Elicit reasons for their answers to Exercise 3.

Expansion/Homework

(1) You may want to bring in different English/English dictionaries that are suitable for your students such as the *Longman Dictionary of American English*. Discuss the advantages and the disadvantages of bilingual vs. monolingual dictionaries. (2) Assign the exercises for homework, then discuss, working on pronunciation. (3) After students have completed Exercise 1, you may want to have them work in pairs to learn the vocabulary. One student can ask what a specific word in the reading means; his or her partner answers with a definition he or she has learned from the dictionary.

Link to *NorthStar: Reading and Writing*

If students are also using the companion text, you may want to have them write in a notebook any new vocabulary they have learned in Section 1C of both texts. You may want to have students group these words according to categories you or they have chosen (such as: *what you take with you on a trip, places to stay, places to visit*, and so on).

2 Focus on Listening, PAGE 119

✪✪✪ A LISTENING ONE: *An Unusual Vacation*

Suggested Time: 10 minutes ⏱

Focus

To establish the context and tone of the telephone hotline conversation to which students will listen; to introduce the speakers; to elicit predictions about the content (save these on the board for Listening for Details section).

Setup

Have students read the questions, then listen to the first part of the segment and answer the questions. Students can compare their answers to those of a partner or read them out loud to the class.

✪✪✪ LISTENING FOR MAIN IDEAS

Suggested Time: 10 minutes ⏱

Focus

To help students listen for the main ideas in the telephone conversation.

Setup

Have the students read the sentences, then mark the answers True or False as they listen. To help concentration, invite students to close their eyes during some of the listening. Have students read their answers to a partner, then check them as a class.

Expansion/Homework

You may want to have students correct the false sentences.

✪✪✪ LISTENING FOR DETAILS
Suggested Time: 15 minutes ⏲

Focus
To get students to listen carefully, this time for specific information.

Setup
First, have students read the lists silently. Then answer any questions they may have and play the listening again. Students can mark their answers, then read what they have checked off to a partner. If disagreements arise, replay the segment rather than simply giving the answer. Have students compare their earlier predictions to the actual text.

Expansion/Homework
You might want to have students work as a class. During the second listening, stop after every two or three items. Elicit reasons for choices.

✪✪ REACTING TO THE LISTENING
Suggested Time: 15 minutes ⏲

Focus
To encourage students to make inferences based on information about the Ice Hotel from the listening.

Setup
For Exercise 1, have students read the questions for Excerpt One. Then play the excerpt. Do the same for Excerpt Two. Probe the reasons for students' choices. Make sure students understand how meaning is expressed through tone of voice. For Exercise 2, give students time to read the questions and think about their answers. Discuss as a class.

Expansion/Homework
You may want to further the discussion by having students work in pairs to make a list of what they would bring to the Ice Hotel. Pairs can read their lists to the class. Write down all items on the board. Then tell students they can only bring ten items. In small groups, they can work together to decide what those ten items would be. To ensure a lively discussion, insist that groups reach a consensus.

✪✪✪ B ▌ LISTENING TWO: *Vacations around the World*
Suggested Time: 15 minutes ⏲

Focus
To introduce other ideas for vacations; to have students practice listening to short descriptions.

Setup

Invite students to read the different travel brochures, then listen to the tape about three vacations described in them. Have students check their answers by working in pairs, then listen again to do Exercise 3.

Expansion/Homework

Bring in any travel brochures you think might interest students, perhaps about local activities. Have them read the brochures for information about the activities they could do at the places described.

Link to *NorthStar: Reading and Writing*

If students are also using the companion text, you may want to put students in small groups and ask them to choose one of the four locations discussed in the listening/speaking text (Sweden's Ice Hotel; Southern California USA; Nepal; Bali, Indonesia) and then, using the information from the reading/writing text have them devise a route to this location from where they are now that does not rely on air travel. *How many different modes of transportation would you need? About how long would it take to get there? Would that be a pleasant journey?* Share highlights with the class.

✪✪✪ C   LINKING LISTENINGS ONE AND TWO

Suggested Time: 15 minutes 🕐

Focus

To get students to make distinctions among the vacation spots mentioned in the listening, and to express opinions about the spots.

Setup

Have students answer individually, then work in small groups (of different cultural backgrounds, if possible) to share their answers. Small groups can report the highlights of the discussion to the class, which you can then note on the board.

Expansion/Homework

(1) You may want to have students prepare their answers for homework, then report their answers to the class and discuss their opinions. (2) Ask students which places would be most interesting/least interesting to them and why. (3) Have students research further information about one of the places listed. How much would it cost to fly there? To stay there? and so on.

Link to *NorthStar: Reading and Writing*

If students are also using the companion text, you may want to have them integrate ideas from Unit 8 of that text in any further research they do. For example, *How can you get to Southern California without flying? To the Himalayas? To Bali?*

❸ Focus on Vocabulary, PAGE 122

✪ EXERCISE 1
Suggested Time: 15 minutes ⏲

Focus
To reinforce definitions of unit vocabulary.

Setup
Have students complete the exercise individually, then compare their answers with those of a partner.

Expansion/Homework
(1) For further practice, have students look at the brochures in Section 2 and discuss what they would do in each of the places, using the vocabulary in these exercises. (2) Have students complete this at home and discuss the answers in class.

✪ EXERCISE 2
Suggested Time: 10 minutes ⏲

Focus
To reinforce definitions of unit vocabulary.

Setup
Have students complete this exercise on their own and check their answers with the class.

Expansion/Homework
This, too, can be completed at home and discussed in class.

✪ EXERCISE 3
Suggested Time: 15 minutes ⏲

Focus
To reinforce unit vocabulary by using it in conversation.

Setup
Have students work in pairs completing the exercise. You should circulate to correct usage and pronunciation errors.

Expansion/Homework
Have students bring in pictures of different vacation spots. Have them look at the pictures and describe activities people can do there.

✪ EXERCISE 4
Suggested Time: 15 minutes ⏲

Focus
To reinforce unit vocabulary by using it in a group discussion.

Setup

Put students in groups of three or four and ask them to take turns responding to the statements. They can then share the highlights of their discussion with the class. You should monitor pronunciation of vocabulary and *can/can't*.

Expansion/Homework

Ask students to write one or two sentence responses to the questions for homework. They can discuss their answers in small groups in class.

 For extra vocabulary practice, have students work on the self-grading vocabulary activities for the unit on the NorthStar Companion Website at **http://www.longman.com/northstar.**

4 Focus on Speaking, PAGE 124

A   PRONUNCIATION: *Can* and *Can't*

Suggested Time: 20 minutes

Focus

To help students learn how the modals *can* and *can't* are stressed; to practice saying *can* and *can't* in sentences about travel.

Setup

Have students listen to the examples on the tape. Then have students listen again and complete the exercises, discussing the answers as a class. In Exercise 5, have students practice reading the sentences from Exercise 4 in pairs. Circulate as necessary to help with pronunciation and appropriate stress.

Expansion/Homework

After students complete Exercise 4, have them brainstorm other sentences with *can* and *can't* about the vacation spots featured in Section 2. Write them on the board. Then have students practice pronouncing these sentences as well.

B   STYLE: Making Polite Requests

Suggested Time: 20 minutes

Focus

To give students language for and practice in making polite requests.

Setup

Have students read the introductory paragraph silently. Read the chart aloud. Have pairs of students (of different fluency levels) do the following information-gap activity. Note that the information that Student B will need to complete the activity is on page 164.

Expansion/Homework

To extend students' awareness of polite requests beyond the theme of the unit, have them write down a list of requests they routinely make of other classmates and people they see every day. For example, requests related to classroom activities, shopping, the post office, and so on. Then have them practice making these requests politely.

Link to *NorthStar: Reading and Writing*

If students are also using the companion text, you may want to have students identify the polite requests in the grammar box in Section 4B of that text and explain to them that *could* is also used to express ability or possibility.

✪✪ C   GRAMMAR: *Can* and *Can't*

Suggested Time: 25 minutes 🕙

Focus

To have students work on usage of *can* and *can't* for ability and possibility in the context of vacations.

Setup

For Exercise 1, have students read the examples, then answer the questions. Ask students to read the grammar box silently. For Exercise 2, have students prepare questions to ask two other classmates about what they can do. As students prepare questions, walk around the room to assist as needed. For Exercise 3, put students in pairs (sitting next to each other) to talk about what you can and can't do at Quebec's Ice Hotel.

Expansion/Homework

(1) For Exercise 2 encourage students to vary how they present the information; for example, Miguel can dance. Both Miguel and Hiroshi can dance. Hiroshi can ice skate, but Miguel can't, and so on. (2) As a follow-up to Exercise 3, have students make statements about the vacation spots highlighted in Section 2: the Himalayas, Southern California, and Bali. (3) For further practice, offer exercises from *Focus on Grammar, Basic* and from *Basic English Grammar*. See the Grammar Book References on page 167 of the Student Book for specific units and chapters.

Link to *NorthStar: Reading and Writing*

If students are also using the companion text, have them read sentences with *can* and *can't* in Section 4B of that text out loud. Write them on the board. Use these sentences and sentences from this section, 4C, to practice appropriate stress of *can* and *can't* from Section 4A.

 For extra listening practice, have students use the NorthStar Companion Video.

✪✪✪D SPEAKING TOPIC

Suggested Time: 25–30 minutes

Focus
To extend students' ability to talk about vacation places and to make polite requests.

Setup
Have students work in pairs (of different cultural backgrounds, if possible) to read the directions, fill in the chart, and perform the role play. Circulate to assist with any language issues that may arise.

Expansion/Homework
(1) You may want to assign the preparatory work for homework. (2) You may want to audio- or videotape conversations to use as an error-correction exercise or errors can be noted on a piece of paper for later discussion (see page vii). (3) You may want to have students who come from the same countries work together to prepare information about popular vacation spots in their countries. Encourage them to bring in pictures of these areas.

Link to *NorthStar: Reading and Writing*
If students are also using the companion text, you may want to have them use the information from Section 4D of that text as the basis for another role play.

✪E RESEARCH TOPIC

Suggested Time: 30–50 minutes in class, 1–2 hours outside

Focus
To get students to use community resources to gather information about a place they want to visit.

Setup
Help students find information. Have them prepare their reports at home. Encourage them to bring in pictures, posters, or postcards of the place they are talking about.

Expansion/Homework
(1) After the reports have been presented, you may want to have students ask questions. Distribute some questions on index cards to get started. (2) You may want students to write a paragraph for Step 2.

Staying Healthy

OVERVIEW	
Theme:	Health and Illness
Listenings:	Listening One: *Thin-Fast* (a radio commercial)
	Listening Two: *Health Problems and Remedies* (two conversations)
Critical Thinking Skills:	Interpret a cartoon
	Assess personal health practices
	Infer word meaning from context
	Distinguish between opinion and fact
	Rank student findings
Listening Tasks:	Listen and predict
	Listen and identify main ideas
	Listen for supporting details
	Characterize speaker's tone
	Listen to and take notes on conversations
	Compare and contrast information from both listenings
	Listen to and take notes on student commercials
	Listen to and comment on student reports
Speaking Tasks:	Brainstorm healthy practices
	Make predictions
	Express opinions
	Use new vocabulary in an open conversation
	Express concern about health problems
	Give and receive advice
	Role-play a radio commercial
	Interview people on health practices
	Report research findings
Pronunciation:	Rhythm: content words and highlighting
Vocabulary:	Word definitions
	Context clues
Grammar:	*Should, ought to,* and *have to*

UNIT SUMMARY

This unit looks at health: weight-loss strategies, health problems, and natural remedies. Listening One features a radio commercial for a diet product: Thin-Fast Tea. Listening Two involves two short, informal conversations about health problems and natural remedies for these problems.

The companion unit of *NorthStar: Reading and Writing* deals with depression, particularly Seasonal Affective Disorder (SAD) and its treatments.

1 Focus on the Topic, PAGE 131

✪✪✪A PREDICTING

Suggested Time: 10 minutes ⏱

Focus
To get students thinking about what people do to stay healthy and lose weight.

Setup
After students look at the pictures and the title of the chapter, have them think about the questions before discussing their answers as a class. As students answer the questions, write their answers on the board to encourage broad participation and appropriate vocabulary.

Expansion/Homework
(1) Have students work in pairs or share their answers in small groups, then report their ideas to the class. (2) Have students write the answers, then share them in pairs or with the class.

Link to *NorthStar: Reading and Writing*
If students are also using the companion text, you may want to have them look at the picture in Section 1 of that text. Discuss the idea of mental health versus physical health.

✪✪B SHARING INFORMATION

Suggested Time: 20 minutes ⏱

Focus
To discover students' awareness of healthy versus unhealthy activities; to discuss their personal health habits.

Setup
Have students work in small groups (of different cultural backgrounds, if possible) to complete the lists, then discuss the questions about the activities listed.

✪✪✪C **PREPARING TO LISTEN**

BACKGROUND
Suggested Time: 15 minutes ⏲

Focus
To give students information about weight and health in the United States; to get students thinking about ways to lose weight.

Setup
Have students read the information about weight and health. Answer any questions. Have students discuss the answers to the questions as a class.

Expansion/Homework
(1) You may want to have students complete this exercise as homework. Then discuss it in class. (2) If time permits, have students discuss experiences they have had or that friends or family members have had with any of these weight-loss strategies.

VOCABULARY FOR COMPREHENSION
Suggested Time: 15 minutes ⏲

Focus
To introduce vocabulary and concepts related to weight-loss and health in preparation for the listening.

Setup
Have students read the sentences and match the definitions individually, then compare their answers with a partner (of similar fluency).

Expansion/Homework
(1) Assign as homework. Correct and work on pronunciation in class. (2) You may want to have students work in pairs to learn the vocabulary. Student A can ask what a specific word in the sentences means; Student B answers from the list of definitions. To add challenge, tell Student B not to look at the list. (3) As homework, you may want to have students write sentences using the new vocabulary.

Link to *NorthStar: Reading and Writing*
If students are also using the companion text, provide them with a list of the words from that unit, and as a class discuss which words from that list might be useful in a discussion of weight and health. List these on the board and encourage students to use these words in their small group discussions throughout this unit.

2 Focus on Listening, PAGE 134

✪✪✪ A | LISTENING ONE: *Thin-Fast*

Suggested Time: 10 minutes ⏲

Focus
To establish the context and tone of a radio commercial; to introduce the speakers; to elicit predictions about the listening (multiple possibilities).

Setup
Have students read the questions, then listen to the first part of the segment and answer the questions. Students can share their answers with a partner or with the class.

✪✪✪ LISTENING FOR MAIN IDEAS

Suggested Time: 10–15 minutes ⏲

Focus
To help students listen for the main ideas of the radio commercial about Thin-Fast.

Setup
Have the students read the sentences, then circle the answers as they listen. To help concentration, invite students to close their eyes during some of the listening. Have students compare their answers with those of a partner, then check them as a class.

✪✪✪ LISTENING FOR DETAILS

Suggested Time: 15 minutes ⏲

Focus
To get students to listen again, this time for specific information.

Setup
First, have students read the sentences, filling in the answers they already know. Then play the commercial again and have students compare their answers with those of a partner. If disagreements arise, replay the segment rather than simply giving the answer. Have students return to the beginning of Section 2 to revisit their predictions.

Expansion/Homework
You may want to have students correct the false statements.

✪✪ REACTING TO THE LISTENING

Suggested Time: 20 minutes ⏲

Focus
To encourage students to make inferences based on tone of voice and word choice; to encourage students to listen beyond the literal meaning of the words.

Setup

For Exercise 1, have students read the paragraph about commercials and the list of strategies. Discuss these as a class. Answer any vocabulary questions. Then have students listen to the excerpts and mark their answer; discuss with the class. For Exercise 2, make sure students understand the distinction between opinion and fact. Then have them complete the exercise and discuss their answers with a partner. For Exercises 3 and 4, discuss as a class. Probe for reasons for students' choices.

Expansion/Homework

Exercises 2, 3, and 4 can be assigned for homework and discussed in class.

Link to *NorthStar: Reading and Writing*

If students are also using the companion text, ask them to consider this question: *As you have learned in this unit, Americans are very concerned about their weight. Many people even say they are depressed because they are 10 or 15 pounds overweight. Using the information you have learned in Unit 9 from both texts, discuss in small groups why being overweight might cause people to feel depressed. Are they really depressed? What is the cure?*

✪✪✪ B   LISTENING TWO: *Health Problems and Remedies*

Suggested Time: 15 minutes 🕒

Focus

To introduce the context of the second listening segment; to give practice listening to informal conversations.

Setup

Invite students to talk about the pictures as a class. Then have them listen to the tape and answer the questions. They can compare their answers with those of a partner. If any disagreements arise, play the tape again so students can correct their own answers.

Expansion/Homework

You may want to have students listen to the tape once and then complete the exercise as a class. Write their answers on the board, including blanks and question marks for omitted or incorrect information. They can listen to the tape again to confirm their answers.

✪✪✪ C   LINKING LISTENINGS ONE AND TWO

Suggested Time: 15 minutes 🕒

Focus

To get students to compare and to express opinions about the health problems and the remedies featured in the two listening segments.

Setup

Have students discuss their answers in small groups, then report the highlights of their discussions to the class, which you can note on the board.

Expansion/Homework

(1) Work with the whole class, getting students to listen and respond to one another's ideas. Encourage the use of vocabulary from Section 1 by listing it on the board and referring students to it. Correct pronunciation and usage errors orally and on the board. (2) You may want to have students prepare their answers for homework, then report to the class and discuss their opinions.

Link to *NorthStar: Reading and Writing*

If students are also using the companion text, you may want to have them talk about natural and chemical remedies that can alleviate SAD symptoms.

❸ Focus on Vocabulary, PAGE 138

✪ EXERCISE 1
Suggested Time: 10 minutes ⏱

Focus
To work with unit vocabulary in a conversational context.

Setup
Put students in pairs (sitting next to each other) to fill in the blanks. Then they can practice reading the conversation out loud to each other until they are comfortable with their parts. Then have the pairs switch roles.

Expansion/Homework
(1) You may want to divide the class into two groups: one half reads A, the other half reads B. (2) If students need more practice with these words, have them work in pairs to write a conversation using all of the words listed in Exercise 1. Circulate as necessary to correct. Then students can role-play the conversations. (3) This exercise also works well as homework.

✪ EXERCISE 2
Suggested Time: 15 minutes ⏱

Focus
To work with unit vocabulary in a conversational context.

Setup
Have students work in small groups to answer the questions. Groups can then share their answers with the class. You should circulate to help with pronunciation and usage errors.

Expansion/Homework
Ask students to write answers for homework and discuss their answers in small groups in class.

Link to *NorthStar: Reading and Writing*

If students are also using the companion text, have them discuss these questions as well: *What is a <u>common</u> <u>treatment</u> for a cold in your country? In your country, do people discuss their <u>emotional</u> problems with friends? Describe how studying English <u>affects</u> your life.*

 For extra vocabulary practice, have students work on the self-grading vocabulary activities for the unit on the NorthStar Companion Website at **http://www.longman.com/northstar**.

4 Focus on Speaking, PAGE 139

✪✪ A   PRONUNCIATION: Rhythm: Content Words and Highlighting

Suggested Time: 15 minutes 🕐

Focus

To raise awareness of sentence stress and to practice placing stress on the important content words of a sentence.

Setup

Have students read the introductory paragraphs and listen to the examples given. Then have students complete Exercise 1 and show what they have underlined to a partner. Discuss any discrepancies with the class. For Exercise 2, ask students to listen to the sentences to check their answers and practice saying them with a partner. For Exercise 3, have students read the conversations with a partner and underline the highlighted words. In Exercise 4, have students listen to the conversations to check answers from Exercise 3. Then have students practice saying the conversations with a partner giving the highlighted words the appropriate amount of stress. Circulate as necessary to help with pronunciation and appropriate stress.

Expansion/Homework

Refer students to page 179 of the audioscript. Have them mark stress on the sentences of one paragraph, and practice reading the sentences aloud.

Link to *NorthStar: Reading and Writing*

If students are also using the companion text, you may want to have them practice the conversation in Section 4A of that text. Practice the sentences individually, then as a dialog.

✪✪✪ B   STYLE: Expressing Concern, Giving and Receiving Advice

Suggested Time: 20 minutes 🕐

Focus

To help students express concern as well as give and accept advice.

Setup

Read the introductory statement and the chart. Have pairs (of different fluency levels) practice the conversations involving a health problem. When students are comfortable with their conversations, they can choose one to perform for the class.

Expansion/Homework

(1) Bring in (or have students bring in) magazine advertisements for different remedies to help students with their advice to the health problems they discussed in Exercise 3. First have them look at the ads. Answer any questions. (2) You may want to have students work in a fluency line (see page viii). (3) Have one student stand up and present a problem to the class. Each class member offers advice. When that student sits down, another student can stand up.

Link to *NorthStar: Reading and Writing*

If students are also using the companion text, you may want to have them explain to the class the advice given in Section 4A, Exercise 1, of that text.

✪✪ C   GRAMMAR *Should, Ought to, Have to*

Suggested Time: 25 minutes

Focus

To have students discover and practice appropriate uses of *should, ought to*, and *have to* in the context of weight loss.

Setup

For Exercise 1, have students read the examples, then answer the questions. Ask students to read the grammar box silently. For Exercise 2, have them complete the exercise individually and compare their answers to those of a partner. Then have students read the conversation with their partner again.

Expansion/Homework

(1) Have students role play doctor/patient conversations. Give each pair a situation (ailment, patient's attitude) on index cards. Let them practice for a few minutes, then perform for the class. (2) For further practice, offer exercises from *Focus on Grammar, Basic* and from *Basic English Grammar*. See the Grammar Book References on page 167 of the Student Book for specific units and chapters.

Link to *NorthStar: Reading and Writing*

Have students read conversations from both texts out loud (listening/speaking Section 4C, Exercise 2; reading/writing Section 4A, Exercise 4), paying attention to sentence stress as discussed in Section 4A of the listening/speaking text.

 For extra listening practice, have students use the NorthStar Companion Video.

✪✪✪ D   SPEAKING TOPICS

Suggested Time: 20–25 minutes 🕙

Focus
To extend students' ability to talk about remedies, expressing concern, and giving and receiving advice.

Setup
Have students read the directions. Give students, working in pairs (of similar fluency), time to brainstorm ideas. Correct language errors. Students can practice their commercials before reading them to the class.

Expansion/Homework
(1) Bring in magazine ads that would be helpful. Circulate them and answer any content questions that may arise. (2) You may want to audio- or videotape conversations to use as an error-correction exercise. You can transcribe segments (see page vii).

✪ E   RESEARCH TOPIC

Suggested Time: 30–50 minutes in class, 1–2 hours outside 🕙

Focus
To get students to talk with people outside of class about health habits.

Setup
Brainstorm with students about who they could interview about health habits. Have students work in pairs (of opposite genders, if possible) to write interview questions, conduct interviews, and report back to the class.

Expansion/Homework
(1) You may want to have students work on developing the questions as a class. Students can first write down a few questions on their own. As they share them with the class, write them on the board. Then students can choose a few of the questions. (2) You may want to have students create a chart to use for filling in information. On a piece of paper, students can write the names of the people across the top of the page and the questions in a list down the left side. They should fill in the chart with the answers to the questions. This format can be useful for comparing answers. (3) When students share the results of their interviews with the class, encourage them to use appropriate adverbs and expressions of frequency as discussed in Unit 6, Section 4C.

Link to *NorthStar: Reading and Writing*
If students are also using the companion text, you may want to have them write a brochure about Thin-Fast, using the brochure in Section 4D as a model.

Endangered Languages

OVERVIEW

Theme:	Endangered Languages
Listenings:	Listening One: *Language Loss* (a class session) Listening Two: *My Life, My Language* (an autobiographical account)
Critical Thinking Skills:	Infer information not explicit in the text Support opinion with reasoning Hypothesize reasons Correlate specific examples to broad themes Summarize main ideas Summarize and evaluate student findings
Listening Tasks:	Listen and predict Listen and identify main ideas Listen for details Interpret speaker's tone Link information from two texts using a graphic organizer Relate listening to personal values Listen to and take notes on student explanations
Speaking Tasks:	Share background information Make predictions Express opinions Give examples to explain a general statement Survey classmates Interpret statistics Report findings on an endangered language
Pronunciation:	Using contractions with *will*
Vocabulary:	Word definitions Context clues Editing inaccurate definitions
Grammar:	Future with *will*

UNIT SUMMARY

This unit is about endangered languages. Listening One is a teacher giving a lecture on endangered languages. Listening Two is a woman talking about her experience with an endangered language, Maori, and what she is doing to preserve it.

The companion unit of *NorthStar: Reading and Writing* deals with endangered cultures—what makes cultures endangered and what some people are doing to prevent cultures from dying.

1 Focus on the Topic, PAGE 147

✪✪✪A PREDICTING

Suggested Time: 10 minutes

Focus
To get students thinking about language and the idea that some languages may become endangered and die.

Setup
After students read the title and study the pictures, have them think about the questions before discussing them as a class. Make sure students understand key words, such as *endangered*. As students answer the questions, write their answers on the board to encourage broad participation.

Expansion/Homework
Have students work in pairs or share their answers in small groups, then report their ideas to the class.

✪✪B SHARING INFORMATION

Suggested Time: 10 minutes

Focus
To discover students' own language backgrounds and experience.

Setup
Divide the students into groups of four. Ask students to read and then discuss the questions. Discuss the interesting highlights with the class. Who in your class speaks the most languages?

Expansion/Homework
(1) Have students write answers for themselves, then report to the group.
(2) Consider these follow-up questions: *Does anyone in the class (or does a family member of anyone in the class) speak an endangered language? What is it? Why is it endangered?*

Link to *NorthStar: Reading and Writing*
If students are also using the companion text, ask them to consider the languages of the endangered cultures they discussed in Section 1B.

✪✪✪ C PREPARING TO LISTEN

BACKGROUND
Suggested Time: 15 minutes ⏱

Focus
To give students some facts about languages and what is happening to them worldwide.

Setup
Have students read the questions and mark the answers to their best guesses. Answer any vocabulary questions that arise. Then have students read the information and check their answers. Which piece of information was the most surprising? Discuss the information as a class.

Expansion/Homework
(1) This can be done for homework and followed by a class discussion. (2) Have students answer the questions in pairs.

VOCABULARY FOR COMPREHENSION
Suggested Time: 15 minutes ⏱

Focus
To introduce vocabulary and ideas related to endangered languages in preparation for listening.

Setup
Have students read the sentences and match the definitions individually. Then pairs (of different fluency levels) can share their answers. Discuss as a class and go over pronunciation.

Expansion/Homework
(1) Assign as homework. Elicit answers and comments in class. (2) After students have completed the exercise, you may want to have them work in pairs to learn the vocabulary. One student can ask what a specific word from the statements means; his or her partner provides the definition.

Link to *NorthStar: Reading and Writing*
If students are also using the companion text, provide them with a list of the vocabulary items from Section 1C from both texts. Ask them to look at the words from both texts. Which words from the reading/writing text are good words to use in the discussion of endangered languages (*roots, unique, survive, environment, ancestors, nomadic, destroy, mainstream*)? Which words from the listening/speaking text are good words to use in a discussion of endangered cultures (*endangered, extinct, communities, powerful, replaced, preserve, native language, bilingual*)?

2 Focus on Listening, PAGE 150

✪✪✪ A | LISTENING ONE: *Language Loss*
Suggested Time: 10 minutes ⏱

Focus
To establish the context and tone of the lecture; to introduce the speakers; to elicit predictions about the content (endangered languages—why they become endangered and what some people do to prevent them from becoming extinct).

Setup
Have students read the questions, then listen to the first part of the segment and answer the questions. Students can read their answers to a partner or read them out loud to the class. Elicit several possibilities for question 3 and reasons for these choices.

✪✪✪ LISTENING FOR MAIN IDEAS
Suggested Time: 10 minutes ⏱

Focus
To help students listen for the main ideas of the lecture.

Setup
Have the students read the statements, then mark them as True of False as they listen. To help concentration, invite students to close their eyes during some of the listening. Have students compare their answers to those of a partner, then discuss them as a class.

Expansion/Homework
Ask students to think about the answers that they marked false. Why are they false? Ask students to change the false statement to make it a true statement.

✪✪✪ LISTENING FOR DETAILS
Suggested Time: 15 minutes ⏱

Focus
To get students to listen carefully again, this time for specific information presented in the lecture.

Setup
First, have students read the questions, marking the ones they already know. Play the listening again, having students mark their answers as they listen. Have students compare their answers with those of a partner. If disagreements arise, replay the segment again rather than simply giving the answer. Encourage students to give reasons for their answers.

Expansion/Homework
Have students complete this exercise with a partner.

✪✪ REACTING TO THE LISTENING
Suggested Time: 15 minutes 🕐

Focus
To encourage students to make inferences based on tone of voice and word choice and to encourage students to share their own reactions to the material in the listening.

Setup
For Exercise 1, have students read the questions, then listen to Excerpt One. Elicit the answer to question 1, then elicit various answers to question 2. Focus students' attention on how tone of voice affects meaning in English. Then move on to Excerpt Two. Probe for reasons. For Exercise 2, give students time to read the questions and think about their answers. Then have students discuss the questions in small groups.

Expansion/Homework
(1) For Exercise 1, answer questions as a class. (2) Have students write down their answers for Exercise 2 at home and be prepared to discuss their answers in class.

✪✪✪ B LISTENING TWO: *My Life, My Language*
Suggested Time: 15 minutes 🕐

Focus
To expand the theme by listening to a Maori woman talk about what she is doing in her family and community to preserve the Maori language.

Setup
Play the tape and invite students to circle the answer that best answers each question. Walk around the room and assist as needed. Discuss answers as a class.

Expansion/Homework
You may want to have students listen to the tape once and then complete the exercise as a class. Write their answers on the board. They can listen to the tape again to confirm their answers.

✪✪✪ C LINKING LISTENINGS ONE AND TWO
Suggested Time: 15 minutes 🕐

Focus
To get students to identify specific ideas from Listening Two that could be examples of a larger idea from Listening One.

Setup
First ask students to complete the chart on their own. Then divide the class into pairs to discuss their answers. Encourage students to write their own sentences of examples that might fit in the chart. Have students share the highlights of their discussion with the class, which you can note on the board.

Expansion/Homework

(1) Work with the whole class, getting students to listen and respond to one another's ideas. Encourage the use of vocabulary from Section 1 by listing it on the board and referring students to it. Correct pronunciation and usage errors orally and on the board. (2) You may want to have students prepare their answers for homework, then report to the class and discuss their opinions.

Link to *NorthStar: Reading and Writing*

If students are also using the companion text, you may want to have them create a similar chart with information from Reading Two in Unit 10. For example, you could provide them with some general ideas such as: *nomadic way of life*; *bad effects of logging on the Penan way of life.*

3 Focus on Vocabulary, PAGE 154

✪ EXERCISE 1
Suggested Time: 15 minutes

Focus
To work with unit vocabulary in fixing sentences where the words are used incorrectly.

Setup
Have students (of different fluency levels) work in pairs. Have students read and discuss the problems with each sentence. Together have them change words in the sentence to make it correct.

Expansion/Homework
This exercise works well as homework. Discuss answers in class.

✪ EXERCISE 2
Suggested Time: 15 minutes

Focus
To practice unit vocabulary by discussing answers to open-ended questions about the listening.

Setup
Have students work in small groups taking turns asking and answering the questions. Circulate to help answer any questions and to correct any usage or pronunciation errors.

Expansion/Homework
Students can write answers to these questions for homework.

Link to *NorthStar: Reading and Writing*
If students are also using the companion text, provide them with the vocabulary list from Unit 10 of that text and ask them to look at their questions from Section 3, Exercise 3, of that text. Have students choose any questions from this list that they think would contribute to the group discussion they are having with this exercise.

 For extra vocabulary practice, have students work on the self-grading vocabulary activities for the unit on the NorthStar Companion Website at **http://www.longman.com/northstar**.

4 Focus on Speaking, PAGE 155

✪✪A PRONUNCIATION: Using Contractions with *Will*
Suggested Time: 15 minutes

Focus
To practice speaking using the contracted form of *will*.

Setup
Have students listen to the examples given. Then have students listen to Exercise 1 and repeat the lines. Then have students practice saying the sentences with a partner. For Exercise 2, have students work in pairs. Student A asks a question using the contracted form of *will* when he or she can. Student B selects the right answer from the list and reads the response, using the contracted form of *will* when he or she can. Circulate as necessary to help with pronunciation and appropriate stress.

✪✪✪B STYLE: Giving Examples
Suggested Time: 20 minutes

Focus
To help students develop conversational skills by providing specific examples to support general statements.

Setup
Read the introduction and chart about general statements and examples. For the following information-gap activity, have students work in pairs. Student A looks at this page, Student B refers to page 165. Students ask the questions listed on their page and use the information provided to answer these questions trying to practice the phrases they studied in this section. You should circulate to help correct pronunciation or phrasing errors.

Link to *NorthStar: Reading and Writing*

If students are also using the companion text, you may want to have them write questions for a partner about endangered cultures modeled on these questions about endangered languages. (For example: *Are there many endangered cultures?*) Have students exchange papers with their partner and then use these phrases and the ones suggested in Section 4A of the reading/writing text to write answers.

✪✪C GRAMMAR: Future with *Will*

Suggested Time: 25 minutes 🕐

Focus

To have students practice using *will* when talking about future events.

Setup

In Exercise 1, have students read the example, then answer the questions. Next they can read the grammar box silently. Clear up any misunderstandings and then have students work in groups of three to complete the chart in Exercise 2. Walk around and cue students to correct their own errors in grammar, vocabulary, pronunciation, and intonation. Discuss answers as a class.

Expansion/Homework

(1) Have students write 4–5 questions about what might happen to English because of the Internet. For example: *Will English become the world language? Will English adopt words from other languages more or less because of the Internet?* Have students read their questions to each other and discuss the answers paying special attention to the contracted *will*. (2) In pairs, have students tell each other what they think will happen to their native language in their lifetime. Have them listen carefully checking for errors with the gerunds and infinitives. (3) For further practice, offer exercises *from Focus on Grammar, Basic* and from *Basic English Grammar*. See the Grammar Book References on page 167 of the Student Book for specific units and chapters.

Link to *NorthStar: Reading and Writing*

If students are also using the companion text, have them revisit Section 4B, Exercise 3, from the reading/writing text. Have students write four sentences about the Maori language using *will* in the future.

 For extra listening practice, have students use the NorthStar Companion Video.

✪✪✪D SPEAKING TOPICS

Suggested Time: 30 minutes 🕐

Focus

To extend students' ability to talk about the future of endangered languages, making general statements and giving examples.

Setup

For Step 1, have students read the directions for this section, then divide them into pairs. Students take turns asking and answering the questions using the information provided. You should circulate and help correct usage, pronunciation, grammar, and phrasing errors. For Step 2, have the pairs discuss their answers to these questions. Each student takes notes on what his or her partner says using the chart provided. Share the highlights of these discussions with the class.

Expansion/Homework

These activities would also work well as small group discussions. For Step 1, have students take turns asking and answering the questions. While students are asking or answering, the other students listen for errors and point them out to the speakers. As a group, decide how to correct any errors that arise.

Link to *NorthStar: Reading and Writing*

If students are also using the companion text, you may want to have them discuss in small groups Topics 1 and 2 from Section 4C. Encourage students to use vocabulary from both units when discussing these questions and to pay close attention to their use of future with *will*.

✪E   RESEARCH TOPIC

Suggested Time: 30–50 minutes in class, 1–2 hours outside 🕙

Focus

To get students do research on the Internet or in a library about endangered cultures and languages.

Setup

Brainstorm with students additional language or cultural groups as well as researching strategies such as KEY WORDS for Internet and library searches. Send students out to get the information requested. In class, have students present information on the language group they chose.

Expansion/Homework

You might ask students to write up the results of their research for homework.

Link to *NorthStar: Reading and Writing*

If students are also using the companion text, this section fits well with Section 4D in the reading/writing text. Have students find the answers to all the questions from both texts when sent off to do their research. Their reports will have more depth and variation if these two sections are combined.

Student Book Answer Key

UNIT 1

BACKGROUND

1 **page 2**

(*top*): mountain-climbing guide, animal trainer, private detective; (*bottom*): cartoon artist, astronomer, professional basketball player

VOCABULARY FOR COMPREHENSION, page 4

1. e
2. i
3. a
4. c
5. g
6. h
7. d
8. f
9. j
10. b

A LISTENING ONE, page 5

1. b
2. a
3. b
4. a
5. Answers will vary.

LISTENING FOR MAIN IDEAS, page 5

1. b
2. b
3. c
4. a
5. b

LISTENING FOR DETAILS, page 6

1. T
2. T
3. F
4. T
5. T
6. F
7. T
8. F

REACTING TO THE LISTENING

1 **page 6**

Excerpt One

1. a; Her tone of voice: she sounds excited.
2. b; He interrupts her.

Excerpt Two

1. a; His tone of voice: he sounds sarcastic.
2. b; His tone of voice: he sounds amused.

Excerpt Three

1. b; His tone of voice: he sounds as if he is joking.
2. b; He is chuckling.
3. a; He sounds in earnest. He gives a straight answer.

B LISTENING TWO

1 **page 7**
Answers will vary.

2 **page 7**

(left): 1; (right): 2

3 **page 8**

a. 1, 2
b. 1
c. 1
d. 1
e. 2
f. 2
g. 1
h. 2
i. 1, 2
j. 1, 2

3 FOCUS ON VOCABULARY

1 **page 9**

1. offbeat
2. helping other people
3. get started
4. to work outdoors
5. quit
6. high-paying
7. tiring
8. be careful
9. lucky

2 **page 10**
Suggested answers:

1. You want to work outdoors then. OR You don't like working indoors.
2. Me neither. That's an offbeat job.
3. Congratulations! You were lucky to get the job.
4. Yes, you need to be careful. OR Yes, I think it 's very tiring.
5. So you don't know how to get started?
6. That sounds like the right job for you then. OR So you don't like working alone.
7. Me too. I'd love such a high-paying job. OR Me too. I have such a low-paying job.
8. You sound very creative.
9. I agree. I think mountain-climbing is too dangerous. OR Mountain-climbing guides are very adventurous.
10. Teaching is the right job for you.

A PRONUNCIATION

1 **page 12**

1. 3; <u>da</u>ngerous
2. 3; im<u>por</u>tant
3. 3; re<u>la</u>xing
4. 4; <u>e</u>ducated
5. 3; ar<u>tis</u>tic
6. 2; <u>pa</u>tient
7. 4; un<u>u</u>sual
8. 3 or 4; <u>in</u>teresting

2 **page 12**

1. private de<u>tec</u>tive
2. <u>win</u>dow washer
3. high <u>sal</u>ary
4. <u>taste</u> buds
5. <u>ice</u> cream
6. spicy <u>foods</u>
7. de<u>part</u>ment store

3 **page 12**

1. b
2. e
3. h
4. d
5. f
6. g
7. a
8. c

C GRAMMAR

2 page 14

Suggested answers:

1. A mountain-climbing guide's job is / isn't tiring.
2. An ice-cream taster is / isn't a creative person.
3. A professional basketball player's work is / isn't difficult.
4. Private detectives are / aren't patient people.
5. Window washing is / isn't an interesting job.
6. Animal training is / isn't important work.
7. A professional shopper's job is / isn't relaxing.

UNIT 2

BACKGROUND

2 page 19

1. F; Urban greening programs bring the country to the city.
2. F; The first city gardens grew vegetables.
3. T
4. F; Community gardens grow vegetables and flowers for the neighborhood people who work in the gardens.

VOCABULARY FOR COMPREHENSION, page 19

1. i	4. h	7. a	10. f
2. b	5. d	8. g	
3. j	6. e	9. c	

A LISTENING ONE, page 21

1. b   2. c   3. Answers will vary.

LISTENING FOR MAIN IDEAS, page 21

Check: 1, 2, 4

LISTENING FOR DETAILS, page 21

1. T	4. F	7. T	10. T
2. F	5. T	8. T	
3. T	6. T	9. F	

REACTING TO THE LISTENING

1 page 22

Excerpt One

1. c   2. b   3. a

Excerpt Two

1. b   2. b

B LISTENING TWO

1 page 23

Answers will vary.

2 page 23

1. neighbors
2. on the roof
3. picking up garbage

3 FOCUS ON VOCABULARY

1 page 24

1. d		5. e
2. f		6. c
3. h		7. a
4. g		8. b

2 page 25

1. urban greening		5. empty lot
2. get together		6. hang around
3. roof garden		7. grow up
4. relax		

A PRONUNCIATION

1 page 27

a. 3		d. 2	
b. 2		e. 1	
c. 1		f. 3	

2 page 27

/əd/	/t/	/d/
planted	worked	played
wanted	walked	removed
	liked	lived
	watched	stayed

B STYLE, page 28

1. too		5. either
2. either		6. too
3. too		7. either
4. either		8. too

C GRAMMAR

2 page 31

1. started	5. decided	9. sold
2. wanted	6. got	10. bought
3. cleaned	7. planned	11. bought
4. picked up	8. raised	12. were

UNIT 3

VOCABULARY FOR COMPREHENSION, page 39

1. b	4. a	7. a
2. a	5. b	8. a
3. a	6. a	9. a

A LISTENING ONE, page 40

1. b
2. c
3. Answers will vary.
4. Answers will vary.

LISTENING FOR MAIN IDEAS, page 40

1. T   2. F   3. F   4. T

LISTENING FOR DETAILS, page 41

A. do
B. provide
C. fixing, music
D. (1) earn, represent; (2) equal
   Example: three, one, saved
E. walking

REACTING TO THE LISTENING

1 page 42

Excerpt One

1. b
2. His tone of voice: he sounds disappointed.
3. He doesn't want to trade services. He would like to trade things.

Excerpt Two

1. a
2. Her tone of voice: she sounds excited.
3. She's always wanted to learn how to play the piano.

Excerpt Three

1. b
2. His tone of voice: he is whining.
3. He feels he doesn't have any skills to exchange. He doesn't know how to do anything.

B LISTENING TWO

1 and 2 page 43

Picture A:	Conversation 3	a jacket	$75
Picture B:	Conversation 1	a camera	$200
Picture C:	Conversation 2	a lamp	$50

3 FOCUS ON VOCABULARY

1 page 44

1. used
2. cheap
3. regular price
4. exchange
5. a good deal
6. stuff
7. compare
8. unusual
9. valuable

A PRONUNCIATION

1 page 47

1. 13   3. 50   5. 70   7. 19
2. 40   4. 16   6. 18

3 page 47

1. $7.50   3. $319.40   5. $1,500
2. $83.25   4. $16.99

UNIT 4

VOCABULARY FOR COMPREHENSION, page 55

a. 5   d. 1   g. 10   j. 3
b. 4   e. 6   h. 2
c. 8   f. 7   i. 9

A LISTENING ONE, page 56

1. b   2. a   3. Answers will vary.

LISTENING FOR MAIN IDEAS, page 56

Check: 1, 3, 5, 7, 9

LISTENING FOR DETAILS, page 57

1. F   5. T
2. F   6. F
3. F   7. T
4. T   8. T

REACTING TO THE LISTENING

1 page 57

Excerpt One

1. a   2. "Huh."

Excerpt Two

1. a   2. "Really! Interesting."

B LISTENING TWO

2 page 58

Answers will vary.

3 page 58

1. in the sewer pipe
2. the owners and people from a company
3. to save the dog

4 page 58

1. The woman wants to save the dog. The man doesn't care.
2. Answers will vary.

3 FOCUS ON VOCABULARY

1 page 60

1. hero
2. companion
3. safe
4. trained
5. get my attention
6. owns
7. saves
8. caught on fire

2 **page 61**

Suggested answers:

1. Oh, yes. She has a service dog.

2. Her house caught on fire?

3. I'm glad everyone was safe.

4. No. How did her dog get her attention?

5. Yes. Service dogs are trained well.

6. Yes. She is lucky to own one.

7. Yes, the dog is a good companion.

8. He saved her!

9. Yes. Kimba is a hero.

A PRONUNCIATION

1 **page 62**

1. What do service animals do?

2. What do hearing dogs do?

3. Where do deaf people use hearing dogs?

4. Why do deaf people use hearing dogs?

5. What do you think about hearing dogs?

B STYLE

2 **page 63**

1. a	3. a	5. a
2. a	4. b	6. b

C GRAMMAR

3 **page 65**

Suggested answers:

1. Where do puppies live?
   Puppies live with trainers.

2. What do puppy trainers do?
   Trainers teach basic behavior.

3. What do service dogs do?
   Service dogs help open and close doors, turn lights on and off, and pick up things from the floor.

4. What do facility dogs do?
   Facility dogs work with health professionals. They help teach patients how to do things.

5. What does CCI do?
   CCI trains service dogs and gives them to people who need assistance in the United States.

6. When do puppies start training?
   Puppies start training when they are 15 months old.

7. When do people get service dogs?
   People get service dogs after they are trained.

8. When do service dogs retire?
   Service dogs retire after eight years.

9. Who does CCI give dogs to?
   CCI gives dogs to people who need assistance in the United States.

10. Why does a puppy live with a trainer?
    A puppy lives with the trainer to learn basic behavior.

UNIT 5

VOCABULARY FOR COMPREHENSION, page 72

1. a	4. a	7. a	10. a
2. a	5. b	8. b	
3. a	6. b	9. b	

A LISTENING ONE, page 73

1. b	2. b	3. Answers will vary.

LISTENING FOR MAIN IDEAS, page 73

1. pro	2. con	3. con	4. pro
5. pro			

LISTENING FOR DETAILS, page 74

1. c	2. a, b, c	3. b, d	4. c
5. c			

REACTING TO THE LISTENING

1 **page 75**

Excerpt One

1. Terry doesn't think talking and driving is a good idea.

2. He chides Caller 1, saying: "So you're one of those people who talks and drives . . . hmmm."

Excerpt Two

1. Terry doesn't think people should talk on the phone in restaurants.

2. His tone of voice: he sounds as if he doesn't approve, as if he is catching Caller 2 doing something wrong. He forces Caller 2 into admitting she is in a restaurant.

B LISTENING TWO, page 76

E-mail One

1. b	2. b

E-mail Two

1. b	2. a

E-mail Three

1. c	2. a

3 FOCUS ON VOCABULARY

1 page 77

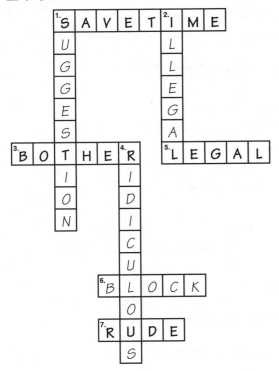

A PRONUNCIATION

2 page 79

1. a. Student A
   b. Student B
2. a. Student B
   b. Student A
3. a. Student A
   b. Student A
4. a. Student A
   b. Student B

C GRAMMAR

2 page 81

1. to do
2. talking, to talk
3. answering
4. overhearing, to overhear
5. to turn off
6. to come
7. watching
8. to use
9. to use
10. having, to have

UNIT 6

VOCABULARY FOR COMPREHENSION, page 87

a. 3   c. 7   e. 6   g. 1
b. 4   d. 2   f. 5

A LISTENING ONE, page 88

1. b   2. b   3. Answers will vary.

LISTENING FOR MAIN IDEAS, page 88

a. 1   b. 2   c. 4   d. 3

LISTENING FOR DETAILS, page 88

1. a   4. a   7. b   10. b
2. b   5. a   8. a
3. a   6. a   9. a

REACTING TO THE LISTENING

1 page 89

Excerpt One

1. a
2. Her tone of voice: she sounds surprised.
3. She expected to meet a woman, since most nannies are women.

Excerpt Two

1. a
2. Her tone of voice: she sounds surprised.
3. Few people—men or women—like doing household chores.

Excerpt Three

1. b
2. His tone of voice: he sounds embarrassed and hesitant.
3. He has to admit that the husband didn't like having another man living in the house, being often alone with the wife.

B LISTENING TWO

1 page 90

Conversation 1: firefighter

Conversation 2: elementary school teacher

Conversation 3: auto mechanic

2 page 90

Conversation 1: Men. You have to be strong.

Conversation 2: Both. Children should have men and women as role models. Boys need to know they can be teachers when they grow up.

Conversation 3: Both. If the woman mechanic can do the job, that's all she (the woman speaking) needs.

3 FOCUS ON VOCABULARY

☐ page 91

1. typical
2. have a problem with
3. is good at
4. get along
5. hire
6. breaks down
7. role model
8. to tell you the truth

A PRONUNCIATION

☐ page 94

1. a; rising intonation
2. b; falling intonation
3. b; falling intonation
4. a; rising intonation
5. a; rising intonation
6. b; falling intonation

UNIT 7

VOCABULARY FOR COMPREHENSION

☐ page 101

1. a
2. a
3. b
4. a
5. a
6. b
7. b
8. a

A LISTENING ONE, page 103

Answers will vary.

LISTENING FOR MAIN IDEAS

☐ page 103

1. T
2. F
3. T

LISTENING FOR DETAILS, page 103

Larry

1. nervous
2. chili peppers
3. relaxed

Dan

1. miserable
2. chocolate, wheat flour
3. With chocolate: in love, upbeat
   With wheat flour: relaxed, upbeat

Barbara

1. stressed
2. turkey, orange juice
3. With turkey: energetic
   With orange juice: energetic, upbeat

REACTING TO THE LISTENING

☐ page 104

Excerpt One

1. a; His tone of voice: he sounds pleased. Also, he asks what's in it.

2. b; He says, "Wow!" and sounds surprised.

Excerpt Two

1. b; Her tone of voice: she sounds angry.

2. b; She says to him, "Are you crazy?"

B LISTENING TWO, page 104

Kate

1. excited, nervous
2. She's getting married.

Derek

1. stressed out
2. He has a lot to do.

Jane

1. irritable
2. She was woken up by someone having the wrong number.

Jeff

1. miserable
2. He failed a math test.

3 FOCUS ON VOCABULARY

☐ page 106

Be: alone, angry, bad, crazy, delicious, good for you, hot, in a bad mood, in a good mood, in a hurry, rude, stupid, stressed

Feel: alone, angry, bad, crazy, hot, stupid, stressed

Look: angry, bad, crazy, delicious, hot, stupid, stressed

Made with: chili peppers, turkey

Smell: bad, delicious

Taste: bad, delicious, hot

A PRONUNCIATION

☐ page 107

good [ʊ]	mood [uw]
look	soon
cook	cool
could	soup
would	Luke
cookies	too
book	news
	food
	juice
	noon
	fruit

4 **page 108**

1. S   3. D   5. S   7. D
2. S   4. D   6. D   8. S

5 **page 108**

1. b   3. d   5. a
2. c   4. f   6. e

B STYLE

1 **page 109**

Waiter/Waitress	Customer
3	6
5	2
1	4

C GRAMMAR

3 **page 112**

A: Do we need any rice?
B: Yes, we need some rice.

A: Do we need any chili peppers?
B: No, we don't need any chili peppers.

A: Do we need any flour?
B: Yes, we need some flour.

A: Do we need any bananas?
B: Yes, we need some bananas.

A: Do we need any milk?
B: Yes, we need some milk.

A: Do we need any coffee?
B: No, we don't need any coffee.

A: Do we need any apples?
B: No, we don't need any apples.

A: Do we need any bread?
B: Yes, we need some bread.

A: Do we need any sugar?
B: No, we don't need any sugar.

A: Do we need any carrots?
B: No, we don't need any carrots.

A: Do we need any orange juice?
B: Yes, we need some orange juice.

A: Do we need any soup?
B: No, we don't need any soup.

UNIT 8

VOCABULARY FOR COMPREHENSION

2 **page 118**

cross-country skiing: Picture 4
dogsledding: Picture 3
snowmobiling: Picture 2
snowshoeing: Picture 1

3 **page 118**

Cross out:

1. lodging   3. inn
2. sleeping bag   4. hotel

A LISTENING ONE, page 119

1. b   2. a   3. c   4. a
5. Answers will vary.

LISTENING FOR MAIN IDEAS, page 119

1. F   3. F   5. F
2. T   4. F   6. T

LISTENING FOR DETAILS, page 120

Things in the Ice Hotel

Check: 1, 2, 3, 4, 7

Things near the Ice Hotel

Check: 2, 3, 4, 5

REACTING TO THE LISTENING

1 **page 120**

Excerpt One

1. ice and snow   2. b   3. a

Excerpt Two

1. three hours   2. a   3. b

B LISTENING TWO

2 **page 121**

Brochure A: Vacation 2
Brochure B: Vacation 1
Brochure C: Vacation 3

3 **page 121**

Brochure A

Go hiking, swimming
Enjoy views
Meet other travelers
Lodging: camping
Time of year: spring or fall

Brochure B

Visit Disneyland
Take a tour of Hollywood
Go sightseeing, shopping
Visit art museums
Lodging: four nights at the Disneyland Hotel
Time of year: anytime

Brochure C

Relax on the beach
Study history, culture, art, and dance
Learn how to cook Balinese food
Lodging: with a family
Time of year: August or December

3 FOCUS ON VOCABULARY

1 **page 122**

1. g	4. b	7. c
2. h	5. a	8. e
3. i	6. d	9. f

2 **page 123**

Indoor activities

stay at youth hostels

Outdoor activities

go cross-country skiing
go hiking
go to amusement parks
look at the scenery
relax on the beach

Indoor or outdoor activities

have fun
take a tour

A PRONUNCIATION

3 **page 124**

1. Negative	4. Negative
2. Negative	5. Affirmative
3. Affirmative	6. Affirmative

4 **page 125**

1. You can't go ice fishing.
2. You can't go shopping.
3. You can visit an old church.
4. You can't go in the summer.
5. You can go to a museum.
6. You can go cross-country skiing.

UNIT 9

VOCABULARY FOR COMPREHENSION, page 133

1. d	5. j	9. a
2. g	6. h	10. k
3. e	7. i	11. c
4. b	8. f	

A LISTENING ONE, page 134

1. a	2. b	3. Answers will vary.

LISTENING FOR MAIN IDEAS, page 135

1. b	2. c	3. c	4. b
5. a			

LISTENING FOR DETAILS, page 135

1. F	4. T	7. T
2. F	5. F	8. T
3. T	6. T	9. T

REACTING TO THE LISTENING

1 **page 136**

Excerpt 1: a, b, d
Excerpt 2: a, b, e
Excerpt 3: c, e
Excerpt 4: a, b, e

2 **page 136**

1. Fact	3. Opinion	5. Opinion
2. Fact	4. Opinion	6. Fact

B LISTENING TWO, page 137

Conversation One

1. The man is sick. He has a stomachache.
2. Peppermint tea.
3. No. He wants to get some medicine.

Conversation Two

1. The woman is sick. She has a cold.
2. Garlic.
3. Yes. She'll try garlic pills.

3 FOCUS ON VOCABULARY

1 **page 138**

1. terrible	6. take care of yourself
2. herbal	7. terrific
3. remedy	8. side effects
4. prevent	9. amazing
5. product	

A PRONUNCIATION

2 **page 140**

1. Thin-Fast is <u>amazing</u>! It <u>really</u> works!
2. It's made from <u>100 percent natural herbs</u>.
3. You just drink <u>one</u> cup of Thin-Fast <u>twice</u> a day.
4. You <u>don't</u> have to exercise, and you <u>don't</u> have to go on a diet.
5. You can eat fattening foods <u>every day</u>, and you'll <u>never</u> gain weight.
6. I lost <u>65</u> pounds in only <u>three</u> months.
7. Now I'm <u>thin</u> and <u>happy</u>.

4 **page 141**

1. A: What kind of <u>tea</u> are you drinking?
   B: <u>Thin-Fast</u> tea.
2. A: Should I drink it <u>three</u> times a day?
   B: No, you should only drink it <u>twice</u> a day.
3. A: Which <u>flavor</u> do you <u>prefer</u>?
   B: I like the <u>orange</u> flavor.
   A: <u>Really</u>? I prefer the <u>lemon</u> flavor.
4. A: <u>Garlic</u> is really <u>good</u> for your <u>health</u>.
   B: <u>Really</u>? But garlic is so <u>bad</u> for your <u>breath</u>.
   A: Not if you take garlic <u>pills</u>.

5. A: These chili peppers are <u>delicious</u>. I <u>love</u> chili peppers.
   B: I like them, <u>too</u>, but I <u>can't</u> eat them. They <u>always</u> give me a <u>stomachache</u>.
   A: <u>Really</u>? That's <u>too bad</u>. You could try drinking <u>peppermint tea</u>. It's <u>very good</u> for stomachaches.

C GRAMMAR

2 page 144

1. shouldn't
2. have
3. ought
4. Should
5. don't have to
6. shouldn't
7. should

UNIT 10

VOCABULARY FOR COMPREHENSION, page 149

1. f
2. j
3. h
4. g
5. a
6. c
7. b
8. e
9. d
10. i

A LISTENING ONE, page 150

1. a
2. c
3. Answers will vary.

LISTENING FOR MAIN IDEAS, page 150

1. T
2. F
3. T

LISTENING FOR DETAILS, page 150

1. b
2. c
3. b
4. b
5. c
6. b
7. b
8. b

REACTING TO THE LISTENING

1 page 151

Excerpt One

1. No.
2. The student says, "Why is it important? . . . Doesn't everything die?"

Excerpt Two

1. Yes.
2. Yes.
3. The student sounds concerned and asks if people are doing anything else to save dying languages.

B LISTENING TWO, page 152

1. a
2. b
3. a
4. a
5. b
6. b
7. a
8. b

3 FOCUS ON VOCABULARY

1 page 154

1. ~~Children~~ [People don't] speak dead languages [anymore].
2. Endangered languages will probably [not] survive a long time.
3. An extinct language is [not] spoken by many people.
4. Linguists study cultures and ~~places~~ [languages].
5. A community is a group of people who have ~~nothing~~ [many things (a lot)] in common.
6. Sometimes the language of a ~~less~~ [more] powerful community replaces the language of a ~~more~~ [less] powerful community.
7. People who grow up in the United States speak ~~Chinese~~ [English] as a native language.
8. Linguists want to preserve languages because they ~~don't~~ want others to learn them.
9. Linguists worry that endangered languages ~~won't~~ [will] disappear and be forgotten.
10. ~~Spanish~~ [English] is the official language of the United States.

A PRONUNCIATION

2 page 156

1. b
2. e
3. c
4. g
5. a
6. d
7. f

Unit Word List

The **Unit Word List** is a summary of key vocabulary from the Student Book's Vocabulary for Comprehension and Focus on Vocabulary sections. The words are presented by unit, in alphabetical order.

Unit 1

adventurous
be careful
contestant
creative
dangerous
factory
flavor (noun)
get started
help other people
high-paying
host (noun)
indoors
insurance policy
low-paying
lucky
offbeat
quit
safe (adjective)
spicy food
taste (verb)
taste buds
the right job for someone
tiring
usual
work alone
work outdoors

Unit 2

community garden
drugs
empty lot
garbage
get together (verb)
grow
grow up
hang around
nature
plant (verb)
relax
remove
roof garden
the country
urban greening
yard

Unit 3

a good deal
cheap
compare
earn
equal
exchange (verb)
member
on sale
provide
regular price
represent
service (noun)
skills
spend
stuff (noun)
unusual
used
valuable

Unit 4

alarm (noun)
assist (verb)
catch on fire
companion
deaf
get someone's attention
hearing dogs
hero
own (verb)
owner
safe (adjective)
save
save someone's life
service animals
sound
train (verb)

Unit 5

block (verb)
bother
common courtesy
convenient
distracting
illegal
law
legal
overhear
pay attention
private
public place
ridiculous
right (noun)
rude
save time
suggestion

Unit 6

be good at something
break down (verb)
childcare
childcare workers
get along
have a problem with
hire
household chores
nanny
role model (noun)
to tell someone the truth
training (noun)
typical

Unit 7

alone
angry
chili peppers
crazy
delicious
energetic
good/bad for you
in a good/bad mood
in a hurry
in love
irritable
made with
miserable
nervous
relaxed
smell
stressed
stupid
turkey
upbeat

Unit 8

adventurous	lodging
amusement park	museum
art gallery	relax
beach	scenery
campsite	ski
church	sleeping bag
cross-country skiing	snowmobiling
dogsledding	snowshoeing
go (cross-country) skiing	stay at a place
guest	take a tour
have fun	tourist
hiking	traveler
hotel	youth hostel
inn	

Unit 9

amazing	prevent
artificial	product
calories	remedy (noun)
fattening foods	side effect
go on a diet	take care of oneself
herbal	terrible
herbs	terrific
natural	

Unit 10

bilingual	linguist
community	native language
dead language	official language
disappear	powerful
endangered	preserve
extinct	replace

Introduction to Achievement Tests

The following reproducible Achievement Tests allow teachers to evaluate students' progress and to identify any areas where the students might have problems in developing their listening and speaking skills. The Achievement Tests should be given upon completion of the corresponding Student Book unit.

Description   There are two Achievement Tests for each unit. **Test 1** is a "paper and pencil" test of receptive skills. It assesses students' mastery of listening comprehension and of the vocabulary, pronunciation, and grammar points introduced in the unit.

Test 2 is intended to assess the students' productive, or speaking, skills. It consists of a speaking task related to the content of the unit. Each speaking task is designed to elicit a speech sample lasting several minutes.

Administration   Administration of **Test 1** requires use of the recorded material on the audio CD packaged with this Teacher's Manual. Students will need to listen to the audio program in order to answer the questions in each section of the test. The answer key to the tests and the audioscript of the material on the CD are included at the end of the Achievement Test section.

Teachers can decide how to incorporate **Test 2** (the speaking task) into their testing situations. Some teachers will assign each speaking task immediately after students complete **Test 1**; others may decide to set aside another time to complete it. The tasks may be set up for pairs, small groups, the whole class, or on a teacher-to-student basis. When set up for pairs or small groups, teachers will need to circulate around the classroom and spend enough time with each pair or group to evaluate the production of individual students.

Some teachers may not find it possible to evaluate all of the students on every speaking test. As an alternative, teachers may choose to evaluate only part of a class on a given **Test 2** speaking task and evaluate the remaining students on tests given at a later time. Teachers may also choose to evaluate students only on every other test or on a total of three or four tests over the term.

Scoring Test 1   Individual test items are worth one point, for a maximum total of 30 points per test. To facilitate scoring, an answer key is provided at the end of the book. A student's score can be obtained by adding together the number of correct items. To obtain an overall "listening score" for a student, teachers may average all of the **Test 1** scores that the student received in the class.

Scoring Test 2   Speaking tasks are evaluated holistically using the categories in the rating sheet that follows. The categories include content, vocabulary, pronunciation, and grammar. In each category, 0 indicates poor or inadequate performance for the level; 1 indicates average or acceptable performance; 2 indicates good or outstanding performance. The teacher circles the rating for each category and adds the numbers to obtain a total score out of 8 possible points.

Test 2 Rating Sheet

Student: _____   Unit _____

Content	0	1	2
Vocabulary	0	1	2
Pronunciation	0	1	2
Grammar	0	1	2

Total Score _____

The teacher can complete the rating sheet for each student's test and give it to the student. It can also be kept by the teacher as a record of each student's progress.

An overall "speaking score" for a student may be obtained by averaging all of the **Test 2** scores the student received in the class.

Achievement Tests
Unit 1

Name: _____

Date: _____

TEST 1

A. ☐1 *Listen to the excerpt. Mark the statements **T** (true) or **F** (false).*

_____ **1.** The woman works as a professional shopper.

_____ **2.** The woman does not like to shop.

_____ **3.** Being a professional shopper can be difficult.

_____ **4.** The woman isn't very good with money, so she spends other people's money.

_____ **5.** She got the idea to become a professional shopper when she was working at a department store.

☐2 *Listen to the excerpt again. Number the details (**1–5**) in the correct order.*

_____ **a.** I started to meet people who needed a shopper.

_____ **b.** I quit my job at the department store.

_____ **c.** I started my own business.

_____ **d.** I worked as a salesclerk in a department store.

_____ **e.** I had enough customers to start a business.

B. *Listen to each sentence. Circle the best word or phrase to complete the sentence.*

1. a. an agreement with an insurance company to be paid money in case there is an accident
b. the names and addresses of insurance salespeople

2. a. used only for tasting spicy food
b. parts of the tongue

3. a. plays a game
b. bets money

4. a. different or unusual
b. off the road

5. a. think and do new and different things
b. teach school

6. a. place where you buy things
b. place where things are made

7. a. fun to eat
b. a kind of taste

T1-1

8. **a.** someone who talks to guests on a radio or TV program
   b. someone who plays music

9. **a.** cook food
   b. try food by eating a little bit

10. **a.** food with a boring taste
    b. food with a strong flavor from spices

C. *Listen to each word. Underline the stressed syllable.*

1. cre a tive

2. friend ly

3. de part ment

4. pro fes sion al

5. cus tom ers

6. im por tant

D. *Listen to people talk about their jobs. Circle the sentence that best describes each job or person.*

1. **a.** He is patient.   **b.** He is lucky.
2. **a.** That job is dangerous.   **b.** That job is relaxing.
3. **a.** He has a creative job.   **b.** He has a boring job.
4. **a.** She has an artistic job.   **b.** She has a tiring job.

TEST 2

Topic: Meeting new people at a party

Group activity: You are at a party and meeting some new people. Walk around and ask different people questions.

• What kind of work do they do?

• Do they like their work?

• What interests do they have?

• Express interest in what people say.

• Talk about yourself when people ask you questions.

Achievement Tests
Unit 2

Name: _____

Date: _____

TEST 1

A. ☐1 *Listen to the excerpt. Circle the correct ending for each sentence.*

1. The excerpt is from _____.
   a. a television program
   b. a radio show
   c. an online chatroom

2. The topic of the show is _____.
   a. Talk of the Town
   b. urban greening programs
   c. how to plant a roof garden

3. Today's program had _____.
   a. one caller
   b. two callers
   c. three callers

4. The callers' two ideas for the topic were _____.
   a. house and apartment living
   b. empty lots and neighbors getting together
   c. planting trees and a roof garden

5. The program host _____.
   a. thought both callers had good ideas
   b. didn't like any of the ideas
   c. thought Caller 1 had a better idea than Caller 2

☐2 *Listen to the excerpt again. Mark the statements **T** (true) or **F** (false).*

_____ 1. Both Caller 1 and Caller 2 said they have lots of trees and empty lots in their neighborhoods.

_____ 2. Caller 1 said the neighbors got together to plant seeds.

_____ 3. Caller 1 said one tree was planted in front of each house in the neighborhood.

_____ 4. Caller 2 said she lives in a small apartment building.

_____ 5. Caller 2 goes to the roof garden to relax.

B. *Listen to each sentence. Circle the best word or phrase to complete the sentence.*

1. **a.** an area with no buildings on it   **b.** an old building

2. **a.** things people want   **b.** things people don't want anymore

3. **a.** special spices and herbs   **b.** chemicals that are dangerous

4. **a.** to take the seeds out of the ground   **b.** to put seeds in the ground

5. **a.** not work; have time to rest   **b.** work very hard

6. **a.** leave people   **b.** meet with people

7. **a.** to take away   **b.** to put into the ground

8. **a.** a garden many people grow together   **b.** a garden belonging to one person

9. **a.** to go from place to place   **b.** to stay in one place not doing anything

10. **a.** to become an adult; get older   **b.** to plant vegetables

 C. *Listen to the sentences with past tense verbs. Circle the pronunciation of the verb ending.*

1. **a.** /ɪd/   **b.** /t/   **c.** /d/
2. **a.** /ɪd/   **b.** /t/   **c.** /d/
3. **a.** /ɪd/   **b.** /t/   **c.** /d/
4. **a.** /ɪd/   **b.** /t/   **c.** /d/
5. **a.** /ɪd/   **b.** /t/   **c.** /d/

 D. *Listen to the statements. Circle the correct statement to agree with the speaker.*

1. **a.** I live in a big city too.
   b. I don't live in a big city either.

2. **a.** I don't have a big apartment too.
   b. I don't have a big apartment either.

3. **a.** My apartment building has a roof garden too.
   b. My apartment building hasn't got a roof garden either.

4. **a.** My parents have a farm too.
   b. My parents haven't got a farm either.

5. **a.** I grew up on the farm too.
   b. I didn't grow up on the farm either.

TEST 2

Topic: A favorite park or green area I remember from my childhood

Group discussion: Take turns talking about a park or green area you visited or played at when you were a child.

- Where was the place? When did you go there?

- What other kinds of people went there?

- What did you and the other people do there?

- If one person talks about something that your park had too, tell the group.

Achievement Tests
Unit 3

Name: _____

Date: _____

TEST 1

🎧 **A.** ☐1 *Listen to the conversation. Mark the statements **T** (true) or **F** (false).*

_____ 1. The man is buying a microwave oven on the computer.

_____ 2. The man doesn't like to shop on the Internet.

_____ 3. The woman doesn't shop on the Internet.

_____ 4. After this conversation, the woman will always shop on the Internet.

🎧 ☐2 *Listen to the conversation again. Write **M** for reasons the man likes to shop on the Internet. Write **W** for reasons the woman doesn't like Internet shopping.*

_____ 1. It's easy to compare prices.

_____ 2. You can save money.

_____ 3. It's easier than shopping in stores.

_____ 4. You don't have to leave your house.

_____ 5. I don't like to send credit card information over the Internet.

_____ 6. You can't touch the things before you buy them.

🎧 **B.** *Listen to each sentence. Circle the best word or phrase to complete the sentence.*

1. **a.** member **b.** network
2. **a.** equal it **b.** exchange it
3. **a.** earns **b.** uses
4. **a.** equal **b.** valuable
5. **a.** a good deal **b.** stuff
6. **a.** regular price **b.** sale price
7. **a.** valuable **b.** unusual
8. **a.** equal **b.** exchanged
9. **a.** compared **b.** used

🎧 **C.** *Listen to the prices. Circle the price you hear.*

1. **a.** $15.53 **b.** $50.53
2. **a.** $10.80 **b.** $10.18
3. **a.** $1500 **b.** $500
4. **a.** $60.90 **b.** $16.19

D. *Listen to the statements. Circle the type of statement you hear.*

1. **a.** making a suggestion   **b.** agreeing with a suggestion   **c.** disagreeing with a suggestion

2. **a.** making a suggestion   **b.** agreeing with a suggestion   **c.** disagreeing with a suggestion

3. **a.** making a suggestion   **b.** agreeing with a suggestion   **c.** disagreeing with a suggestion

 E. *Listen to the statements about two apartments. Use the comparative form of an adjective in the list to complete the sentences.*

busy   expensive   big   close

1. The apartment on Main Street is _____ than the apartment on Broadway.

2. The rent for the apartment on Main Street is _____ than the rent for the Broadway apartment.

3. The Broadway apartment is _____ to school than the Main Street apartment.

4. Main Street is a _____ street than Broadway.

TEST 2

Topic: Buying a used car

Role play: Work with a partner. One person is a salesperson, and the other person is a customer.

Customer: You need a new car. You are interested in two different cars.

• Ask questions about each car. Find out how many miles are on the car, how old the car is, what special features it has, and the price.

• Compare the two cars.

Salesperson: Tell the customer about the cars.

• Talk about the year of each car, the miles each has, and how many special features each car has.

• Help the customer compare the cars and decide which car is better for him or her.

Achievement Tests
Unit 4

Name: _____

Date: _____

TEST 1

🎧 **A.** 1 *Listen to the excerpt. Mark the statements **T** (true) or **F** (false).*

_____ 1. The woman is reading a newspaper article to the man.

_____ 2. The man wants to listen to another dog story.

_____ 3. The story is about a dog helping to save a person.

_____ 4. The story has a happy ending.

🎧 2 *Listen to the excerpt again. Number the details **(1–6)** in the correct order.*

_____ 1. The dog fell into an open sewer pipe.

_____ 2. The dog left the house without his owners.

_____ 3. The owners called a company to come out and save the dog.

_____ 4. The owners walked around the neighborhood calling the dog's name.

_____ 5. The city started repairing the sewers on the street.

_____ 6. The owners heard the dog crying.

🎧 **B.** *Listen to the woman telling a story. Circle the correct questions to explain what she wants to say.*

1. a. Do you mean she is blind?   b. Do you mean she is deaf?

2. a. Do you mean service dogs?   b. Do you mean puppy dogs?

3. a. Do you mean safe?   b. Do you mean in danger?

4. a. Do you mean saved?   b. Do you mean trained?

5. a. Do you mean to get their attention?   b. Do you mean to own?

6. a. Do you mean a danger?   b. Do you mean a hero?

🎧 **C.** *Listen to the sentences. Circle the best word or phrase to complete each sentence.*

1. a. people who have something   b. people who have nothing

2. a. noises made in an emergency   b. noises from a party

3. a. things you hear   b. things you see

4. a. to help   b. train

D. *Listen to each sentence. Circle the appropriate follow-up question.*

1. **a.** What kind of animals do you like?
   b. Where do animals live?

2. **a.** What do dolphins eat?
   b. Do you own a parrot?

3. **a.** What is your parrot's name?
   b. How many parrots do you own?

4. **a.** That's an interesting name. What does Lady Squawk-A-Lot do for fun?
   b. Do you like cats?

5. **a.** Oh, no. What do birds eat?
   b. What else does she like to do?

 E. *Listen to the sentences. Circle the appropriate question for each statement.*

1. **a.** Who does he do?   **b.** What do they do?
2. **a.** Where does he live?   **b.** Where do they live?
3. **a.** What does it do?   **b.** What do they do?
4. **a.** When does it start?   **b.** When do they start?
5. **a.** Why do they like the show?   **b.** Why does he like the show?

TEST 2

Topic: Talk about a pet or any other animal you know well.

Pair activity: Work with a partner. Student A will ask questions, and Student B will answer questions about a pet or other animal he or she is familiar with.

Student A: Ask questions about the pet's habits:

• What / it eat?

• Where and when / it sleep?

• What kind of exercise / it need?

Student B: Answer the questions about your pet or an animal you know about. Change roles. Student B asks questions about Student A's animal.

Achievement Tests
Unit 5

Name: _____

Date: _____

TEST 1

A. ☐1 *Listen to the excerpt. Circle the correct ending for each sentence.*

1. Terry, the radio host, is _____.
   a. reading e-mail messages from listeners
   b. listening to callers

2. Mary, the first listener, thinks _____.
   a. people don't know how to be responsible
   b. signs in restaurants will stop rude behavior

3. Alan, the second listener, thinks _____.
   a. we don't need laws about cell phones
   b. we need laws about cell phones and driving

☐2 *Listen to the excerpt again. Mark the statements **T** (true) or **F** (false).*

_____ 1. The e-mail messages make suggestions about how to stop rude cell phone behavior.

_____ 2. Mary thinks people should be responsible and rude.

_____ 3. A quiet car is a train car where you can't use your cell phone.

_____ 4. If you sit in a quiet car on a train, you'll know it will be loud.

_____ 5. Alan thinks using cell phones while driving is dangerous.

_____ 6. Alan agrees with Mary that people can control their own behavior.

B. *Listen to the questions. Circle the appropriate answer for each question.*

1. a. I don't need to stop and find a pay phone. I can make a call from wherever I am.
   b. My parents call me.

2. a. People who always say please and thank you.
   b. People who talk out loud in the movies.

3. a. People waiting in line.
   b. A woman who was holding a cell phone to her dog so it could bark to the person on the other phone.

4. a. Yes, once there were two girls talking about their boyfriends in the line at the grocery store. They didn't know I was listening.
   b. Yes, once I talked to the president of the university. I learned many interesting things.

5. **a.** The worst is when I'm trying to study and my sister is playing loud music.
   b. The worst is when I do one thing at a time.

6. **a.** It bothers me when I see people driving and talking on cell phones.
   b. It bothers me when I'm talking to my best friend.

7. **a.** You can use them to contact people any time and almost anywhere you want.
   b. They don't like listening to other people talking.

8. **a.** I think they are very convenient.
   b. Learn to live with them. They are not going away.

9. **a.** Everyone should use cell phones.
   b. Everyone should be quiet while watching a movie.

10. **a.** Yes, I think that is an important and necessary law.
    b. No, I don't think that's courteous.

C. *Listen to the sentences. Put a check (✓) if you can hear an unstressed **to** in the sentence.*

_____ 1. unstressed *to*

_____ 2. unstressed *to*

_____ 3. unstressed *to*

D. *Listen to the questions. Circle the answers a person who <u>loves</u> cell phones would give.*

1. **a.** I don't mind it.   **b.** I hate it.
2. **a.** I really like it.   **b.** I don't like it.

E. *Listen to the questions. Circle the answers a person who <u>hates</u> cell phones would give.*

1. **a.** I really like it.   **b.** I can't stand it.
2. **a.** It's great.   **b.** It bothers me.

F. *Listen to the speaker. Circle the correct form of the verb to finish each statement.*

1. **a.** calling me
   b. to call me

2. **a.** turning off my cell phone when we go out together
   b. to turn off my cell phone when we go out together

3. **a.** coming home by midnight
   b. to come home by midnight

4. **a.** having his conversation in another room
   b. to have his conversation in another room

TEST 2

Topic: Using cell phones in public

Group discussion: Take turns talking about cell phones.

- What do you like about them?

- What are good reasons for using a cell phone?

- What don't you like about them?

- Do you think we need stronger laws for using cell phones in public? Why or why not?

Achievement Tests
Unit 6

Name: _____

Date: _____

TEST 1

A. ☐1 *Listen to the excerpt. Circle the correct ending for each sentence.*

1. A sitter and a nanny are different. They offer a different kind of _____.
   a. household chore
   b. child care
   c. cleaning service

2. On a typical day, the nanny spends most of his time _____.
   a. cooking
   b. cleaning the house
   c. taking care of the children

3. For this nanny, taking care of the children is _____.
   a. like being a father
   b. a job
   c. not very important

☐2 *Listen to the excerpt again. Mark the statements **T** (true) or **F** (false).*

_____ 1. A sitter usually lives with the family.

_____ 2. A sitter doesn't normally do household chores.

_____ 3. A nanny doesn't always live with a family.

_____ 4. This nanny cooks breakfast, lunch, and dinner.

_____ 5. He always takes the children to school and never picks them up after school.

_____ 6. He normally helps the children do their homework.

_____ 7. He is a nanny for children who don't have a father.

B. *Listen to each sentence. Circle the best word or phrase to complete the sentence.*

1. a. usual
   b. unusual

2. a. to feel confident
   b. to disagree or to not be happy with something

3. a. to like the taste of something
   b. to do something well

4. a. to have a good time; not fight
   b. to go everywhere with another person

5. **a.** to make someone leave their job
   b. to give someone a job

6. **a.** to have an accident
   b. to stop running

7. **a.** a person who shows others new clothes
   b. a good example to other people

8. **a.** education to learn how to do something.
   b. a dog license

9. **a.** the money you pay for rent
   b. work in the house such as cooking and cleaning

10. **a.** taking care of children while parents are not there
    b. cooking

 C. *Listen to the conversations. Circle the best description of the woman's response.*

1. **a.** The woman is surprised.
   b. The woman is going to say more.

2. **a.** The woman is thinking.
   b. The woman wants the man to say more.

3. **a.** The woman is surprised.
   b. The woman is thinking about what the man said.

4. **a.** The woman doesn't believe the man.
   b. The woman wants to say more.

5. **a.** The woman wants more information.
   b. The woman is thinking about it.

 D. *Listen to the questions. Circle the answer that explains how often the nanny or another person does each thing.*

1. **a.** I take them to the movies every day after school.
   b. I take them to the movies about once a week.

2. **a.** Yes, I make breakfast only on Saturdays.
   b. Yes, I make breakfast every morning.

3. **a.** The mother likes to cook dinner but, maybe once a month, she works
   late. I cook when she works late.
   b. The mother works late, so I make dinner Monday through Friday.
   On Saturday, the mom takes the kids out for pizza.

4. a. Yes, he has dinner with the family maybe once a week if they're lucky.
   b. Yes, he's home for dinner with the family at least four nights a week.

5. a. The mother takes the kids to school on her way to work. But if she has a rare early meeting, I take the kids to school.
   b. I take the kids to school, but sometimes the mother has an early meeting and she drops the kids off on her way.

TEST 2

Topic: Women's and men's jobs in the home

Group discussion: Take turns giving your opinions about what jobs men and women should do in the home.

- Are men usually good at cooking or cleaning? Are women better than men at cleaning, cooking, or taking care of children?

- In your home, which jobs do the males in the family normally do? Which jobs do the females normally do?

- Are there any jobs a man or a woman in your culture never do?

Achievement Tests
Unit 7

Name: _____

Date: _____

TEST 1

A. ☐1 *Listen to the excerpt. Mark the statements **T** (true) or **F** (false).*

_____ 1. The radio host is talking to people on the street about food.

_____ 2. The girl's problem is that she is very hungry.

_____ 3. The radio host thinks the sugar in a candy bar will give her energy for the whole day.

_____ 4. The radio host explains why a hamburger and a banana muffin can give her energy.

☐2 *Listen to the excerpt again. Check (✓) all the statements the radio host makes about food.*

_____ 1. Food gives us the energy we need to get through the day.

_____ 2. When you eat sugar, you may feel like you have more energy.

_____ 3. Sugar has lots of vitamins and minerals.

_____ 4. Beef has a lot of iron.

_____ 5. Iron is a mineral that can help you feel more energetic.

_____ 6. Bananas also have a lot of iron.

B. *Listen to the speakers. Circle the response you would give to each person.*

1. **a.** I'm so sorry. You must feel really miserable.
   b. I'm so sorry. You must feel really upbeat.

2. **a.** OK. You sure are irritable today.
   b. OK. You sure are exhausted today.

3. **a.** I wonder why he's so stressed.
   b. I wonder why he's in such a good mood.

4. **a.** You don't need to be nervous. I know you'll do a great job.
   b. You don't need to be angry. I know you'll do a great job.

5. **a.** That is a lot of work. Now I understand why you sound so upbeat.
   b. That is a lot of work. Now I understand why you sound so stressed.

6. **a.** It's irritable. I'm sure you will like it.
   b. It's delicious. I'm sure you will like it.

7. **a.** Don't get so angry at bad drivers, or you will become one of them.
   b. Don't be so relaxed over bad drivers, or you will become one of them.

8. **a.** Now I understand why you look so relaxed.
   b. Now I understand why you look so stressed.

9. **a.** Sounds like you're nervous.
   b. Sounds like you're in love.

10. **a.** I'll call you another time when you are not in a hurry.
    b. I'll call you another time when you are not in a good mood.

C. *Listen to each sentence. Write **S** (same) if the last two vowel sounds are the same. Write **D** (different) if they are different.*

_____ 1.

_____ 2.

_____ 3.

_____ 4.

_____ 5.

D. *Listen to the questions. Complete the answers with a phrase from the list.*

some tuna   some apples   some juice   two pieces of toast   any juice

1. I think we have _____.

2. Yes, you do. We don't have _____.

3. I only had _____.

4. I'd love to have _____.

5. I'd like _____.

TEST 2

Topic: Talk about what foods you like to eat and why.

Pair activity: Work with a partner. Take turns asking and answering questions about your diet.

• What foods do you have in your kitchen now?

• Do any of the foods change the way you feel?

• Which foods give you energy? Which foods have vitamins and minerals?

• Do you eat a healthy diet?

Achievement Tests
Unit 8

Name: _____

Date: _____

TEST 1

A. ☐**1** *Listen to the excerpt. Mark the statements **T** (true) or **F** (false).*

_____ **1.** A representative from the Swedish Tourist Office is speaking.

_____ **2.** There's only one kind of vacation you can take in Sweden.

_____ **3.** Sweden has a lot of nature and many outdoor activities.

☐**2** *Listen to the excerpt again. Check (✓)all the things the speaker says you can see and do in Sweden.*

_____ **1.** Stockholm has museums to visit.

_____ **2.** There's a beautiful fountain on the main street in Stockholm.

_____ **3.** You can see lots of beautiful castles and churches in and around the city.

_____ **4.** There are thousands of lakes in Sweden.

_____ **5.** Sailboating on the ocean is very popular with tourists.

_____ **6.** In winter, people like to ski or ice skate.

_____ **7.** There are lots of old hotels in Stockholm.

B. *Listen to the tourist's questions. Circle the appropriate response to each question.*

1. a. There are many hotels in the city.
   b. There are lots of nice hikes you can take around the city.

2. a. You will want to go to an inn.
   b. You will want to visit our museums.

3. a. Your bed will have a warm sleeping bag.
   b. The beds are made of ice.

4. a. There are some beautiful castles around the city.
   b. There are many modern art galleries in the city.

5. a. The tourist office has information about lodging.
   b. The tourist office has information about city tours.

6. a. You can spend hours on hiking trails in the forest.
   b. You can stay at campsites and sleep outdoors under the trees.

7. a. Your children will really enjoy the amusement park in the city.
   b. Your children will really enjoy the outdoor activities.

8. a. Many young people like to stay at youth hostels.
   b. Many young people like to visit our castles.

9. a. I recommend you take a tour of the sights on our big red tour bus.
   b. You can look at the scenery from the city bus.

10. a. The guided tours on our bus are very informative.
    b. If you are adventurous, I think you should stay at the ice hotel. It's most unusual.

C. *Listen to the sentences. Are they affirmative or negative? Circle the word you hear.*

1. a. can   b. can't
2. a. can   b. can't
3. a. can   b. can't

D. *Listen to the first line of each conversation. Circle the appropriate response.*

1. a. Don't mention it.   b. Certainly. It's on the first floor.   c. Sure, until 5:00.

2. a. Sorry, I don't know.   b. What would you like to know?   c. No, I can't.

3. a. Sorry, it's $35.   b. Certainly. It's $35.   c. No problem.

E. *Listen to the statements. Complete the responses with **can** or **can't.***

1. You mean you _____ drive?

2. Are you saying I _____ stay at the hotel in June?

3. Does this mean I _____ drive your car?

4. Does that mean we _____ ride to the top of the mountain? We don't have to hike to the top?

TEST 2

Topic: Discussing tourist activities

Role play: Work with a partner. One person is the tourist office agent in your hometown. The other person is a tourist asking questions about the town.

Tourist:

- Ask questions about what you can see and do.

- Ask about places to stay, and how much they cost.

Tourist Office Agent:

- Answer the tourist's questions.

- Explain what he or she can and can't do in the area.

Achievement Tests
Unit 9

Name: _____

Date: _____

TEST 1

A. **1** *Listen to the conversation. Circle the correct answer to complete each statement.*

    1. Jack feels _____.
      a. energetic
      b. tired
      c. athletic

    2. The woman suggests that Jack _____.
      a. go to the doctor
      b. go play soccer
      c. take an energy drink

    3. Jack doesn't want to take an energy drink because he read that many of them are _____.
      a. used by a lot of athletes these days
      b. unhealthy
      c. full of the most natural remedies

2 *Listen to the conversation again. Check (✓) all the statements the man and woman have heard or read about the energy drinks.*

    _____ 1. They can pick you up when you are tired.

    _____ 2. They are good for colds.

    _____ 3. They are full of natural ingredients and vitamins.

    _____ 4. You need a doctor's prescription.

    _____ 5. They are full of caffeine and sugar.

    _____ 6. They help you sleep better.

B. *Listen to each statement. Circle the best word or phrase to complete the sentence.*

    1. **a.** diet food
      b. plants used to flavor food or make medicines

    2. **a.** man-made
      b. not man-made

    3. **a.** very bad
      b. normal

    4. **a.** foods that can make you fat
      b. foods that never taste good

5. **a.** something you can take or do to create a health problem
   b. something you can take or do to correct a health problem

6. **a.** to keep from happening
   b. to make worse

7. **a.** an unexpected result that a medicine has on your body
   b. another medicine you must take with the first

8. **a.** very sick
   b. great, wonderful

9. **a.** surprising, unbelievable
   b. confusing

10. **a.** foods that are used in medicine
    b. a measure of the energy in food that the body uses

C. *Listen to each sentence. Circle the stressed words.*

1. The report said that many of those energy drinks are unhealthy.

2. They have a lot of caffeine and sugar.

3. You really shouldn't drink them before you exercise.

D. *Complete the conversation. Number the lines to respond to the speaker's statements.*

_____ **a.** Thanks for the advice. I'll do my best.

_____ **b.** I'm sorry to hear that.

_____ **c.** What's the matter? You sound terrible!

_____ **d.** You should rest and drink lots of liquids.

E. *Listen to each statement. Complete the sentences with the correct form of a modal verb from the list to explain the speaker's sentence.*

| have to | (negative) have to | ought to | (negative) should |

1. With this diet drink, you _____ exercise to lose weight.

2. You _____ have the diet drink with your meals.

3. You _____ drive a car when you take this medicine.

4. John _____ go to the hospital.

TEST 2

Topic: Give advice to someone about how to stay healthy

Pair activity: Work with a partner. Student B will talk about a health problem he or she has, and Student A will express concern and give advice.

Student A:

- Ask Student B what is wrong.

- Express concern, and then give Student B advice about what he or she should and shouldn't do.

Student B:

- Say what is wrong. Explain why you think you have the problem.

- Listen to Student A's advice and respond to it.

Change roles. Student B asks Student A about a health problem and gives advice.

Achievement Tests
Unit 10

Name: _____

Date: _____

TEST 1

A. □1 *Listen to the excerpt. Circle the best word or phrase to complete each statement.*

1. The woman wanted her children to learn _____.
   a. Maori, their native language
   b. English

2. She found schools called "language nests" that teach Maori to children _____.
   a. in pre-school, before they enter school
   b. after the regular school day

3. The language nests were started by _____.
   a. the government
   b. a group of Maori leaders

4. This mother takes Maori language classes _____.
   a. at the language nests
   b. for adults

□2 *Listen to the excerpt again. Mark the statements **T** (true) or **F** (false).*

_____ 1. The government realized the language was dying and brought the idea of the "language nests" to the Maori leaders.

_____ 2. There are only about 700 children bilingual in Maori and English.

_____ 3. Language nests are now a big part of Maori education.

_____ 4. The pre-school language nests meet in neighborhood centers.

_____ 5. The week-long adult classes are completely in Maori. No English is spoken.

B. *Listen to each sentence. Circle the best word or phrase to complete the sentence.*

1. **a.** a dead language   **b.** an official language
2. **a.** linguist   **b.** native speaker
3. **a.** dead   **b.** endangered
4. **a.** replaced them   **b.** preserved them
5. **a.** endangered   **b.** extinct
6. **a.** replace the language **b.** preserve the language
7. **a.** native language   **b.** official language
8. **a.** government   **b.** community

9. **a.** preserve　　　　　　**b.** disappear

10. **a.** bilingual　　　　　　**b.** linguists

 C. *Listen to each sentence. Circle the words you hear.*

1. **a.** What you teach　　　**b.** What'll you teach
2. **a.** Sheila　　　　　　　　**b.** She'll
3. **a.** What you give　　　　**b.** What will you give
4. **a.** she learns　　　　　　**b.** she'll learn
5. **a.** We will　　　　　　　**b.** We'll

D. *Listen to each sentence. Circle the correct word or phrase to complete the sentence.*

1. **a.** survive　　　　　　　**b.** survives
2. **a.** disappear　　　　　　**b.** disappearing
3. **a.** are extinct　　　　　　**b.** will be extinct
4. **a.** they'll　　　　　　　　**b.** they will
5. **a.** she will stay　　　　　**b.** will she stay
6. **a.** won't forget it　　　　**b.** will forget it

TEST 2

Topic:　Are all languages endangered languages?

Group discussion:　Imagine that your native language or a language of a neighboring country is endangered. Take turns talking about how your native language or another language you know of might become extinct.

- What factors might cause the language to die out or disappear?

- Give examples of some languages that have died out or are in danger of dying out. What factors caused them to become extinct or endangered?

- Give examples of things people can do to keep their language alive.

Achievement Tests
Test 1 Audioscript

UNIT 1

A

1 *Listen to the excerpt. Mark the statements **T** (true) or **F** (false).*

I'm a professional shopper. I go shopping for people who are busy and don't have time to shop. People give me a shopping list and some money, and I do the shopping for them. I like my job because I love to shop and I really like to work with people. I'm also very good with money. My job is great, but it isn't that easy. I'm on my feet a lot, so my work is tiring. And it wasn't easy to get started as a shopper. I worked for many years as a salesclerk in a department store. Then I started to meet people who needed a shopper. When I had enough customers, I quit my job at the department store and started my own business.

2 *Listen to the excerpt again. Number the details (1-5) in the correct order.*

B

Listen to each sentence. Circle the best word or phrase to complete the sentence.

1. Mark has an insurance policy for his house. If his house burns down, the insurance company will help pay for his new house. An insurance policy is _____.
2. Spicy foods always burn my mouth because I have sensitive taste buds. Taste buds are _____.
3. Jason wants to be a contestant on a game show. He wants to earn a lot of money. A contestant is someone who _____.
4. She wears funny hats, very big shoes, and baggy pants. Her clothes are offbeat. Something is offbeat when it is _____.
5. The college professor is not at all creative. He always does the same thing over and over again. To be creative is to _____.
6. The sandals were made in a shoe factory. A factory is a _____.
7. She ordered a mushroom pizza because she loves the flavor of mushrooms. A flavor is _____.
8. I really like the host on that radio show. She asks the most interesting interview questions. A host is _____.
9. I'll order the soup and you can taste it. If you like it, you can order a bowl for yourself. To taste is to _____.
10. He likes spicy food so his friends took him to a Thai Restaurant for his birthday. Spicy food is _____.

C

Listen to each word. Underline the stressed syllable.

1. creative
2. friendly
3. department
4. professional
5. customers
6. important

D

Listen to people talk about their jobs. Circle the sentence that best describes each job or person.

1. I taste ice cream all day and I get paid for it!
2. I go high up in the air in a basket to wash the windows on tall buildings.
3. I think of interesting new ice cream flavors to make.
4. As a professional shopper, I'm on my feet all day.

UNIT 2

A

1 *Listen to the excerpt. Circle the correct ending for each sentence*

Host: Good afternoon and welcome to *Talk of the Town.* I'm Juana Ramón. You know, community gardens are one kind of urban greening or urban beautification. Today we want to hear from you, our listeners. What urban greening programs do you see in the city? Let's hear from our first caller. Hello. You're on the air.

Caller 1: Yeah, hi. About five years ago, all the neighbors in my neighborhood got together and planted trees—one tree in front of each house. Now, there are beautiful trees all along the street. The trees make the street shady and cool in the summer, and they make the neighborhood green.

Host: That's a great way to make a city greener. OK. Let's hear from another caller. You're on the air.

Caller 2: Hi. Well, I live in a tall apartment building. There are no empty lots in my neighborhood and there aren't any trees. But we do have a really nice garden on our roof. I really enjoy going there to relax. We have small trees and flowers . . . It's really wonderful.

Host: Roof gardens. What a great idea! Why not plant a garden on top of a building? Well, that's all the time we have this afternoon. Until next week, this is Juana Ramón saying good-bye.

2 *Listen to the excerpt again. Mark the statements **T** (true) or **F** (false).*

B _____

Listen to each sentence. Circle the best word or phrase to complete the sentence.

1. I live in the city. The children play in an empty lot next to the library. An empty lot is _____.
2. They throw away a lot of garbage. Garbage is _____.
3. He is in jail because he sold illegal drugs. Drugs are _____.
4. Every spring we plant flowers in our garden. Plant means _____.
5. I work very hard during the week. I like to relax on the weekend. Relax means _____.
6. This weekend I will get together with my neighbors for a picnic. Get together means _____.
7. We have to remove that big tree because the roots are pushing up the sidewalk. Remove means _____.
8. The city let the neighbors use this empty lot to plant a community garden. A community garden is _____.
9. The older neighbors like to hang around the garden and talk to the gardeners. Hang around means _____.
10. Children who grow up on a farm have a better understanding of nature than city kids do. Grow up means _____.

C _____

Listen to the sentences with past tense verbs. Circle the pronunciation of the verb ending.

1. We visited my uncle's farm. visited
2. We missed his birthday by one day. missed
3. He lived on the farm when he was a boy. lived
4. We looked at the new fence. looked
5. He decided to build it himself. decided

D _____

Listen to the statements. Circle the correct statement to agree with the speaker.

1. I live in a big city.
2. I don't have a big apartment.
3. My apartment building has a roof garden.
4. My parents have a farm.
5. I didn't grow up on the farm.

UNIT 3

A _____

1️⃣ Listen to the conversation. Mark the statements **T** (true) or **F** (false).

Woman: What are you doing?

Man: I'm buying a new camera.

Woman: On the computer?

Man: Yeah, I like to shop on the Internet.

Woman: Oh, yeah?

Man: Sure, Internet shopping is great because it's easy to compare prices, so you can save money. The camera I want costs $800 in the stores, but I found it on the Internet for only $600.

Woman: You got a good deal—you saved $200.

Man: Yeah, and it's a lot easier than shopping in stores. You don't have to leave your house. You just send in your credit card information and they send the stuff to your house.

Woman: That's true—but I'd rather pay cash than use my credit card. And I don't like sending my credit card information over the Internet.

2️⃣ Listen to the excerpt again. Write **M** for reasons the man likes to shop on the Internet. Write **W** for reasons the woman doesn't like Internet shopping.

B _____

Listen to each sentence. Circle the best word or phrase to complete the sentence.

1. I joined a golf club. I can play golf there every day because I am a club _____.
2. I don't like the color of this shirt. Do you have the same one in blue? I don't want to return the shirt. I just want to _____.
3. I think her salary is pretty high. Do you know exactly how much she _____.
4. He is the best worker in this office. Of all the employees, he is the most _____.
5. What? You paid only $5.00 for that lamp? You really got _____.
6. Sorry, there's no discount on this blouse. $45.00 is the _____.
7. She hates wearing the same thing other women are wearing. She always has on something _____.
8. He gets paid the same amount as I do. Our salaries are _____.
9. The salesman told me this toaster was new, but look at the scratches on it. And it looks like there are toast crumbs on the bottom. I think this toaster is _____.

C _____

Listen to the prices. Circle the price you hear.

1. $15.53
2. $10.18
3. $1500
4. $60.90

D _____

Listen to the statements. Circle the type of statement you hear.

1. That's fine with me. Why not?
2. Well, I don't know. I don't think I'll find what I'm looking for there.
3. Why don't we go to the department store?

Listen to the statements about two apartments. Use the comparative form of an adjective in the box to complete the sentences.

1. The apartment on Main Street has four bedrooms, and the apartment on Broadway has only two bedrooms.
2. The rent for the apartment on Main Street is $1000, but the rent for the apartment on Broadway is only $750.
3. The apartment on Main Street is 10 blocks from school and the Broadway apartment is only 3 blocks from school.
4. Every morning at 6 A.M. the traffic starts on Main Street and it's so loud! There is no traffic on Broadway.

UNIT 4

A

1 *Listen to the excerpt. Mark the statements **T** (true) or **F** (false).*

Man: Anything interesting in the paper today?

Woman: Yes. Listen to this . . . "Bandit, a six month-old dog, is safe and happy tonight."

Man: Is this another dog story because I really don't want to hear . . .

Woman: No, no, no. Just listen . . . Bandit, a young, curious dog, wandered off from his home last night, and it seems he fell into an open sewer pipe. The sewer pipes on the street were being repaired. I guess he couldn't get out—he got stuck inside. When he didn't come home, his owners walked all over the neighborhood calling his name. Bandit heard his owners calling his name and got their attention by crying. Finally, his owners figured out where he was. They immediately called a company who came out and was able to save the poor dog. So tonight, he's safe at home again with his owners. What a lucky dog, don't you think?

2 *Listen to the excerpt again. Number the details (1-6) in the correct order.*

B

Listen to the woman telling a story. Circle the correct questions to explain what she wants to say.

1. Did you hear what happened to Mrs. Jones? You know, that lady who can't hear. What's that called when someone can't hear? She's . . . umm.
2. Yes, that's what I mean! And, she has a special dog that helps her. What are those dogs called?
3. Yes. They help people who are deaf or blind. These dogs make sure their owners are . . . What's the word? You know . . . protected from danger?

4. That's it. Well, Mrs. Jones and her dog were walking up the stairs. The dog knows to take care of his owner. The dog learned that at a special school. He was . . .
5. Yes. When the dog hears a sound or thinks there is danger, he was taught to make Mrs. Jones look. You know, to make someone look . . .
6. Yes. Well, there was a strange man next to the stairs and the dog started barking. The man was frightened by the dog and he ran away. The dog saved her from a robber. Why, that dog is a . . . a . . .

C

Listen to the sentences. Circle the best word or phrase to complete each sentence.

1. Dogs can be friends to their owners. They like to be with their owners and follow them around. Owners are _____.
2. When a hearing dog hears an alarm, he immediately gets his owners' attention. Alarms are _____.
3. Hearing dogs tell deaf people about many different sounds; for example, the doorbell ringing or a baby crying. Sounds are _____.
4. Service dogs can assist blind and deaf people in many different ways. Assist means _____.

D

Listen to each sentence. Circle the appropriate follow-up question.

1. I like animals.
2. I really like parrots.
3. Yes, I have one pet parrot.
4. Her name Is Lady Squawk-A-Lot.
5. She loves to watch other birds.

E

Listen to the sentences. Circle the correctly formed question for each statement.

1. Mr. Jones works with dolphins in the dolphin show.
2. The dolphins live in the amusement park.
3. One dolphin jumps through the air.
4. There are two dolphin shows every day: at 10 AM and 2 PM.
5. People like the dolphin show because it is funny.

UNIT 5

A

1 *Listen to the excerpt. Circle the correct ending for each statement.*

Welcome back to *Terry Talks to the Town.* Last week we heard from listeners about rude cell phone behavior. Well, I got several e-mails from listeners with suggestions. This is from Mary in White Plains, New York.

"Hi, Terry. I think theaters and restaurants should just put up a sign that says, 'Please turn off your cell phone.' It seems the best way to me. I think a sign is all we need to control rude cell phone behavior. People should be responsible and polite. I also heard about another great idea called 'quiet cars'—cars on trains where you can't use your cell phone. I think it's good because you know if you sit there, it'll be quiet. These seem like two really good solutions to me." Alan in Seattle, Washington.

"Terry, I think we need laws about cell phones and driving. I think it should be illegal because it's really dangerous. Unfortunately, people can't control their own behavior, or don't have the common courtesy to do it themselves, so we need laws."

☑ 2 Listen to the excerpt again. Mark the statements **T** (true) or **F** (false).

B

Listen to the questions. Circle the appropriate answer for each question.

1. How can a cell phone save you time?
2. Can you give me an example of rude behavior?
3. What is the most ridiculous thing you have ever seen?
4. Have you ever overheard an interesting conversation?
5. What is something that is very distracting for you?
6. Can you tell me something that bothers you?
7. Why do people say cell phones are so convenient?
8. What suggestion do you have for people who don't like cell phones?
9. Can you give an example of common courtesy?
10. It is illegal to drive and talk on the phone in some cities. Do you agree with this?

C

Listen to the sentences. Put a check if you can hear an unstressed to in the sentence.

1. I'm going to use my cell phone.
2. I hate seeing you like this.
3. Let's meet to see a movie.

D

Listen to the questions. Circle the answers a person who loves cell phones would give.

1. How do you like people using cell phones in public places?
2. How do you like the idea of laws against cell phones?

E

Listen to the questions. Circle the answers a person who hates cell phones would give.

1. How do you like people using cell phones in public places?
2. How do you like hearing other people's cell phones?

F

Listen to the speaker. Circle the correct form of the verb to finish each statement.

1. I don't want to see him anymore. But he keeps _____.
2. My boyfriend hates my cell phone. I agreed _____.
3. I won't be late, Mom. I promise _____.
4. I hate to overhear private conversations. So, I asked him _____.

UNIT 6

A

☑ 1 Listen to the excerpt. Circle the correct ending for each sentence.

Host: Why do families hire a nanny? Why not hire a sitter?

Man: A sitter and a nanny are different. For one thing, a sitter *never* lives with the family. Also, a sitter usually doesn't do household chores. A nanny, on the other hand, takes care of the children in the child's home every day. The nanny also usually does some household chores. A nanny usually lives with the family, but not always. It's a different kind of child care.

Host: What is a typical day for you as a nanny?

Man: Well, I usually help the children get ready for school. I help them get dressed, make breakfast and lunch. Sometimes, I take them to school, and I always pick them up after school. I usually help with their homework, and we often play together and things like that.

Host: So, are you like a father to the children?

Man: No, no, no . . . I am not their father. They have a father. He comes home at night. I am a male nanny. I take care of the children when the parents work. It's just my job.

☑ 2 Listen to the excerpt again. Mark the statements **T** (true) or **F** (false).

B

Listen to each sentence. Circle the best word or phrase to complete the sentence.

1. Many jobs, like firefighter or doctor, used to be typical male jobs, but that is changing now. Typical means _____.

2. My father has no problem with me driving his car. He just always wants to be in the car when I'm driving. To have a problem with something means _____.

3. My sister is good at all kinds of sports, and I can't even throw a ball straight. To be good at means _____.

4. Do you and your sister get along, even though you are both so different? To get along means _____.

5. I need a job for the summer. Do you think your dad will hire me in his restaurant? To hire means _____.

6. My car broke down on the way to work yesterday. To break down means _____.

7. My mom is a wonderful role model. I want to be like her: a professional working woman and a loving mother. A role model is _____.

8. Are there any schools that offer training for animal care? I'd like to open a dog salon. Training means _____.

9. I have no time for fun on Saturdays. That's the day I take care of all my household chores. Household chores are _____.

10. I took a childcare class in high school. It helped a lot with my babysitting jobs. Childcare means _____.

C _____

Listen to the conversations. Circle the best description of the woman's response.

1.	(man)	I love doing the housework.
	(woman)	Really?
2.	(man)	Yes, I do the housework every Friday night.
	(woman)	When?
3.	(man)	Friday night, so I have all weekend free.
	(woman)	Hmmmm . . . .
4.	(man)	Come over on Friday and join the fun.
	(woman)	You're kidding . . . .
5.	(man)	Really. I'm having a housework party with music, food, and drinks.
	(woman)	Well . . . .

D _____

Listen to the questions. Circle the answer that explains how often the nanny or another person does each thing.

1. What do you mean you sometimes take the children to the movies?
2. You say you always make breakfast for the children?
3. Why do you only rarely have to make dinner?
4. And the children's father usually gets home before dinner, doesn't he?
5. You say you take the children to school once in a while. Why is that?

UNIT 7

A _____

1 *Listen to the excerpt. Mark the statements **T** (true) or **F** (false).*

Host: Good afternoon and welcome to *Street Talk*. Today, I'm here on Market Street talking to people about food. Food gives us the energy we need to get through the day. But we don't always eat the food that our bodies and minds need. Hi, I'm Marty Moore, the *Street Talk* guy. What's your name?

Jenny: My name's Jenny . . .

Host: Hey Jenny, you look tired. What's the matter?

Jenny: Oh, I was awake all night studying. Now I can't keep my eyes open, I'm so tired.

Host: I see you're eating a candy bar.

Jenny: Yeah, I've always heard sugar gives you energy. I need all I can get today.

Host. Well Jenny, the truth is, when you eat sugar you may feel like you have more energy, but the energy doesn't last. Plus sugar doesn't have any vitamins or minerals, and it's bad for your teeth. Here, I have just the thing for you—a hamburger and a banana muffin.

Jenny: But I said I'm tired, not hungry.

Host: I know that. You see the beef in the hamburger can help you feel more energetic. Beef has a lot of iron. Iron is a mineral that can help you feel more energetic, so you won't feel so tired. And the bananas in the muffin can help you feel better, too. Bananas will help you to feel more energetic.

Jenny: OK, OK, I'll give it a try. Thanks.

2 *Listen to the excerpt again. Check all the statements the radio host makes about food.*

B _____

Listen to the speakers. Circle the response you would give to each person.

1. Oh, no. Things can't get any worse. Yesterday I lost my job and today someone stole my car!
2. Stop bugging me. How many times do I have to tell you I don't want to go to the movies?
3. Look at the boss. He's smiling and singing a song to himself.
4. My knees are shaking. I just can't get in front of everyone and give a speech.
5. I have to finish all this work by Friday. I don't know how I'm going to do it.
6. Fresh mango juice. Hmm . . . I've never tried that.
7. Did you see that driver? He just cut me off! I'm going to follow him.

8. I just got back from a two-week vacation in Hawaii.
9. Tom and I went out on the weekend and had such a great time. He's so wonderful; I really think he's the one.
10. Well, I have to catch my bus in exactly three minutes, so we need to make this fast.

C

*Listen to each sentence. Write **S** (same) if the last two vowel sounds are the same. Write **D** (different) if they are different.*

1. He's a good cook.
2. He's here too soon.
3. He took food.
4. Do you like cool soup?
5. Chocolate is too good!

D

Listen to the questions. Complete the answers with a phrase from the box.

1. Can we make a pie? Do we have any fruit?
2. Do I need to buy something to drink for breakfast?
3. How much bread did you eat?
4. What kind of fish do you want?
5. What would you like to drink?

UNIT 8

A

1 *Listen to the excerpt. Mark the statements **T** (true) or **F** (false).*

Radio Host: Today we're talking with a representative from the Swedish Tourist Office. Tell us, what kind of vacation will I have if I plan a trip to Sweden?

Tourist Rep: Tourists planning a trip to Sweden have many different kinds of vacations to choose from. If you prefer big cities, you may choose to visit Stockholm, Sweden's largest city. In Stockholm, you can visit museums to learn about the local history and culture and go to art galleries to see some Swedish art. There are also some beautiful old churches and castles to visit in and around the city. And of course, as in all big cities, there's lots of shopping and entertainment such as concerts, shows, and restaurants.

Radio Host: And what about for people who love the outdoors?

Tourist Rep: For people who enjoy nature, there's a lot of it in Sweden. Fifty percent of Sweden is covered with forests of beautiful trees, and many wild animals live there. 96,000 lakes and a long range of tall mountains offer tourists lots of opportunities for outdoor activities: swimming, hiking, or relaxing on the beach in summer and skiing or ice skating in winter. It's your choice. And Sweden can make your summer vacation longer because the sun shines almost all day and night. If you can stay awake, it's like doubling your vacation!

2 *Listen to the excerpt again. Check all the things the speaker says you can see and do in Sweden.*

B

Listen to the tourist's questions. Circle the appropriate response to each question.

1. I'm looking for a place to stay. Can you help me?
2. Where can I go to learn about the local history and culture?
3. If the hotel is made of ice, how will I stay warm at night?
4. Where can I find some modern artwork to buy and take home with me?
5. Where can I find out about places to stay in your country?
6. The forests are so beautiful. Can I spend the night there?
7. I have small children. They like going on rides, playing games, and seeing shows. Where can I take them?
8. I'm a college student and don't have a lot of money. Do you have any cheap places for me to stay?
9. When I visit a city for the first time, I like to have a tour guide tell me all about the different parts of the city. What do you recommend?
10. I get bored easily. I always like to try new and unusual things when I go on vacation. What should I do?

C

Listen to the sentences. Are they affirmative or negative? Circle the word you hear.

1. You can go to an art gallery.
2. You can't go there at night.
3. You can hike to the top of the mountain.

D

Listen to the first line of each conversation. Circle the appropriate response.

1. Excuse me. Can you please tell me where the library is?
2. Could you tell me the hours of the bank, please?
3. Would you tell me the price of a theater ticket?

E _____

Listen to the statements. Complete the responses with can *or* can't.

1. I don't have a driver's license.
2. The Ice Hotel is closed in the summer.
3. Here are the keys to my car.
4. This cable car goes to the top of the mountain.

UNIT 9

A _____

1 *Listen to the conversation. Circle the correct answer to complete each statement.*

A: Hi, Jack. How are you?

B: Oh, not great. I'm so tired. I was up all night studying, and now I have to go to soccer practice for the big game tomorrow. (sound sleepy and sluggish)

A: Hey! Why don't you try one of those energy drinks? I hear they can really pick you up when you're tired. They are full of natural ingredients and vitamins. And I heard that they can help you play better at sports. A lot of athletes use them these days. And the great thing is you don't need to go to the doctor. You can just buy them at the market.

B: Well, I heard a report about those energy drinks. It said that many of them are unhealthy. They have a lot of caffeine and sugar, and you really shouldn't drink them before you exercise.

A: Wow, I didn't know that. Then you need to try the most natural remedy.

B: What's that?

A: Sleep!

2 *Listen to the excerpt again. Check all the statements the man and woman have heard or read about the energy drinks.*

B _____

Listen to each statement. Circle the best word or phrase to complete the sentence.

1. My sister buys fresh <u>herbs</u> like parsley and mint, and uses them for cooking. Herbs are _____.
2. I like to use <u>natural</u> products because they have no artificial ingredients. Natural means _____.
3. I have a headache and I feel <u>terrible</u>. Terrible means _____.
4. My favorite foods—chocolate, butter, and cheese—are all <u>fattening foods</u>. Fattening foods are _____.
5. I have a great <u>remedy</u> for stomachaches. It works every time. Remedy means _____.
6. Some people think you can <u>prevent</u> heart attacks by using olive oil in cooking. Prevent means _____.

7. He took headache medicine and it gave him stomachaches. That medicine had very bad <u>side effects</u>. Side effects are _____.
8. My boyfriend has been <u>terrific</u> during my diet. He gives me a rose for every pound I lose. Terrific means _____.
9. Have you seen Marianne? It's <u>amazing</u> how much weight she has lost since the last time I saw her. Amazing means _____.
10. I don't usually eat cake or cookies. They have too many <u>calories</u> for my diet. Calories are _____.

C _____

Listen to each sentence. Circle the stressed words.

1. The report said that many of those energy drinks are unhealthy.
2. They have a lot of caffeine and sugar.
3. You really shouldn't drink them before you exercise.

D _____

Listen to the conversation. Number the lines to respond to each speaker's statement.

1. Hi, How's it going?
2. Oh, I have the flu.
3. I've had it for over a week. Do you know any good remedies?
4. Yes, I've been doing that. You should take vitamins and stay away from people like me so you won't catch it.

E _____

Listen to each statement. Complete the sentences with a modal verb from the box to explain the speaker's sentence.

1. With this diet drink, it's not necessary to exercise to lose weight.
2. We recommend that you have the diet drink with your meals.
3. It's not good to drive a car when you take this medicine. It might make you sleepy.
4. I think John's leg is broken. He needs to go to the hospital.

UNIT 10

A _____

1 *Listen to the excerpt. Circle the best word or phrase to complete each statement.*

Maori is an endangered language, and if children stop learning it, it will die. I decided I wanted my children to learn their native language. I found a pre-school that teaches children Maori before they enter school where they will learn English. The schools are called "language nests." In 1981, a group of Maori leaders saw that Maori was endangered and dying. They decided to do something. They did not want to wait for the government to do anything, so they got together and came up with the idea of pre-schools where children could learn Maori. Now there are over 700 language nests and more than 13,000 children who are bilingual in Maori and English. Language nests are a big part of Maori education.

I also wanted to learn more about my language and culture. Now, there are classes for adults like me. The teachers are all older Maoris, usually grandparents. We meet in neighborhood centers. There are also week-long classes where adults can go and study. In this course, no English is spoken all week! Everything is Maori.

2 Listen to the excerpt again. Mark the statements **T** (true) or **F** (false).

B _____

Listen to each sentence. Circle the best word or phrase to complete the sentence.

1. No one speaks that language anymore. It is _____.
2. That professor has written many articles about language. She is a well-known _____.
3. It had been illegal to teach the Hawaiian language in public schools. In 1987, the government started language programs because so few people knew Hawaiian and the language was _____.
4. Many Native American languages have become extinct because the English language has _____.
5. Another way to say a language is dead is to say it is _____.
6. When a language is endangered, linguists use videotapes, audiotapes, dictionaries and grammar books to try to _____.
7. I was born in Canada and learned to speak French as a child. French is my _____.
8. Linguists say it is important that language is passed on in the home, neighborhood, and _____.
9. Only about 25 percent of people of Maori ethnicity speak Maori. Linguists want children and adults to learn the language so it will not _____.
10. Through the language nests, Maori children learn Maori as well as English. They are _____.

C _____

Listen to each sentence. Circle the words you hear.

1. What'll you teach your children?
2. Sheila goes to the language class on Monday night.
3. What you give will be greatly appreciated.
4. At the language nest program, she'll learn the native language of her grandparents.
5. We'll need to put new tires on that old car.

D _____

Listen to each sentence. Circle the correct word or phrase to complete the sentence.

1. If the language dies, the culture won't _____.
2. If children stop learning it, the language will _____.
3. Linguists predict that in 100 years 90 percent of languages _____.
4. Will they try to save their culture? Yes, _____.
5. Do you know where _____?
6. I'll speak Maori at home so my child _____.

Achievement Tests
Test 1 Answer Key

UNIT 1

A _____

1. a. T   b. F   c. T   d. F   e. T
2.
__2__ a. I started to meet people who needed a shopper.
__4__ b. I quit my job at the department store.
__5__ c. I started my own business.
__1__ d. I worked as a salesclerk in a department store.
__3__ e. I had enough customers to start a business.

B _____

1. a   6. b
2. b   7. b
3. a   8. a
4. a   9. b
5. a   10. b

C _____

1. cre <u>a</u> tive   4. pro <u>fes</u> sion al
2. <u>friend</u> ly   5. <u>cus</u> tom ers
3. de <u>part</u> ment   6. im <u>por</u> tant

D _____

1. b   2. a   3. a   4. b

UNIT 2

A _____

1. 1. b   2. b   3. b   4. c   5. a
2. 1. F   2. F   3. T   4. F   5. T

B _____

1. a   6. b
2. b   7. a
3. b   8. a
4. b   9. b
5. a   10. a

C _____

1. a   2. b   3. c   4. b   5. a

D _____

1. a   2. b   3. a   4. a   5. b

UNIT 3

A _____

1. 1. T   2. F   3. T   4. F
2. 1. M   4. M
   2. M   5. W
   3. M   6. W

B _____

1. a   6. a
2. b   7. b
3. a   8. a
4. b   9. b
5. a

C _____

1. a   2. b   3. a   4. a

D _____

1. b   2. c   3. a

E _____

1. bigger   3. closer
2. more expensive   4. busier

UNIT 4

A _____

1. 1. T   2. F   3. F   4. T
2.
__3__ 1. The dog fell into an open sewer pipe.
__2__ 2. The dog left the house without his owners.
__6__ 3. The owners called a company to come out and save the dog.
__4__ 4. The owners walked around the neighborhood calling the dog's name.
__1__ 5. The city started repairing the sewers on the street.
__5__ 6. The owners heard the dog crying.

B _____

1. b   4. b
2. a   5. a
3. a   6. b

C _____

1. a   2. a   3. a   4. a

D _____

1. a
2. b
3. a
4. a
5. b

E _____

1. a
2. b
3. a
4. b
5. a

UNIT 5

A _____

1️⃣ 1. a   2. b   3. b
2️⃣ 1. T   4. F
   2. F   5. T
   3. T   6. F

B _____

1. a
2. b
3. b
4. a
5. a
6. a
7. a
8. b
9. b
10. a

C _____

✓ 1. unstressed *to*
_____ 2. unstressed *to*
✓ 3. unstressed *to*

D _____

1. a   2. a

E _____

1. b   2. b

F _____

1. a   2. b   3. b   4. b

UNIT 6

A _____

1️⃣ 1. b   2. c   3. b
2️⃣ 1. F   5. F
   2. T   6. T
   3. T   7. F
   4. F

B _____

1. a
2. b
3. b
4. a
5. b
6. b
7. b
8. a
9. b
10. a

C _____

1. a
2. b
3. b
4. a
5. b

D _____

1. b
2. b
3. a
4. b
5. a

UNIT 7

A _____

1️⃣ 1. T   2. F   3. F   4. T
2️⃣ ✓ 1. Food gives us the energy we need to get through the day.
   ✓ 2. When you eat sugar, you may feel like you have more energy.
   _____ 3. Sugar has lots of vitamins and minerals.
   ✓ 4. Beef has a lot of iron.
   ✓ 5. Iron is a mineral that can help you feel more energetic.
   _____ 6. Bananas also have a lot of iron.

B _____

1. a
2. a
3. b
4. a
5. b
6. b
7. a
8. a
9. b
10. a

C _____

1. S
2. S
3. D
4. S
5. D

D _____

1. some apples
2. any juice
3. two pieces of toast
4. some tuna
5. some juice

UNIT 8

A _____

☐1 1. T   2. F   3. T

☐2 ✓ 1. Stockholm has museums to visit.

_____ 2. There's a beautiful fountain on the main street in Stockholm.

✓ 3. You can see lots of beautiful castles and churches in and around the city.

✓ 4. There are thousands of lakes in Sweden.

_____ 5. Sailboating on the ocean is very popular with tourists.

✓ 6. In winter, people like to ski or ice skate.

_____ 7. There are lots of old hotels in Stockholm.

B _____

1. a	6. b
2. b	7. a
3. a	8. a
4. b	9. a
5. a	10. b

C _____

1. a   2. b   3. a

D _____

1. b   2. a   3. b

E _____

1. can't	3. can
2. can't	4. can

UNIT 9

A _____

☐1 1. b   2. c   3. b

☐2 ✓ 1. They can pick you up when you are tired.

_____ 2. They are good for colds.

✓ 3. They are full of natural ingredients and vitamins.

_____ 4. You need a doctor's prescription.

✓ 5. They are full of caffeine and sugar.

_____ 6. They help you sleep better.

B _____

1. b	6. a
2. b	7. a
3. a	8. b
4. a	9. a
5. b	10. b

C _____

1. many, energy drinks, unhealthy
2. lot, caffeine, sugar
3. shouldn't, before

D _____

__4__ **a.** Thanks for the advice. I'll do my best.

__2__ **b.** I'm sorry to hear that.

__1__ **c.** What's the matter? You sound terrible!

__3__ **d.** You should rest and drink lots of liquids.

E _____

1. don't have to	3. shouldn't
2. ought to	4. has to

UNIT 10

A _____

☐1 1. a   2. a   3. b   4. b

☐2 1. F   2. F   3. T   4. F   5. T

B _____

1. a	6. b
2. a	7. a
3. b	8. b
4. a	9. b
5. b	10. a

C _____

1. b	4. b
2. a	5. b
3. a	

D _____

1. a	4. b
2. a	5. a
3. b	6. a